# GAP in (

# 1990-1995

## The First Five Years

by

## William Marshall

ISBN 1-904181-12-0

WRITERSWORLD
15-17 Maidenhead Street
Hertford SG14 1DW
England


www.writersworld.tv

01993 812 500

Writersworld

2 Bear Close

Woodstock        OX20 TJX

# About the author

Bill Marshall was the founding project manager of GAP's China project – all GAP project managers are voluntary – and for a short while he also ran the new Hong Kong project in parallel. In 1995 he handed the lead role to a colleague, but until 1999 kept his oversight over the western provinces of Sichuan and Yunnan, and the four CAAC colleges (see below).

This book, *GAP in China 1990-1995 The First Five Years,* takes the reader through the difficulties of initial negotiation at the time of Tiananmen (1989). With three maritime provinces responding favourably, the first six young GAP volunteers left for China in October 1990, while at the same time, the first six young Chinese teachers arrived in London for their year in the UK. The book continues with the development and build-up of the project over the next five years, not always an easy task.

Keen though he was to entrench each placement in the existing provinces, his constant aim was also to extend GAP to inner provinces, away from the fast developing coastline. Hence the book explores his sorties, first to the ports of Shanghai and Qingdao, and then to Hunan, Sichuan, Yunnan and Hubei; but only in the last was there failure. Marshall also had excellent and fruitful relations with Rolls-Royce plc who – through CAAC, China's air regulatory body – established GAP placements in four prestigious air colleges at Guangzhou, Shanghai, Guanghan (Sichuan) and Tianjin. These colleges regularly supplied sixteen interesting placements a year. GAP-China is grateful for that.

A chapter speaks of initial difficulties in setting up the Hong Kong project in 1991-92. The book continues with a chapter on those Chinese volunteers working in UK institutions and the great difficulties in finding places for them. The writing ends with a chapter recording the reactions of the UK volunteers, first while at work and then ten years later after a decade's reflection.

iii

The book all through exudes an affection for Chinese people, respect for Chinese officials' reliability and an enthusiasm for GAP's work. Today about 100 GAP volunteers a year go to China, in 1990 the total was twelve. The GAP-China and the GAP-Hong Kong projects flourish to this day, but in the first five years there was something special, something of a pioneering spirit that was exhilarating for all.

## Map of China

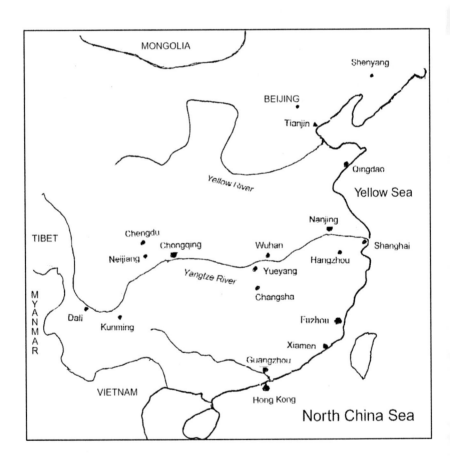

# GAP in China 1990-1995
## The First Five Years

## Contents

## Author's Note

The purpose of this book is not in any way to provide an in-depth study of part of China, or of a prolonged stay in any one town. Nor have I provided more than a few samples of the many tales I heard, for instance, experiences in the Cultural Revolution. It is merely a record, as requested by some GAP-China volunteers. Many I sent to China under the project wrote rich, copious and informative private diaries which would amply supply the wealth of detail and colour needed; I hope some will publish these memories, suitably edited, or at least use them as a basis for other writing. They after all lived and worked there, while I was more or less constantly on the move, a bird of passage twice a year. This book is a report of how the GAP-China project as a whole was established between 1989 and 1995, and of my final years until 1999 as one of the then two project managers.

I have used modern Pinyin spelling for all names of cities, provinces and rivers, with the exception of the River Yangtze and Hong Kong, whose anglicised forms are more familiar. In addition, for simplicity I have used the Pinyin Chinese abbreviation for the names of certain offices:

*jiaowei* (short for the Chinese *jiao yu wei yuan hui*) is easier for us to use than the cumbrous English expression "Education Commission". Many provinces now instead use *jiao yu ting* (Department of Education).

*waiban* (short for *wai shi ban gong shi*) for "the Foreign Affairs Office" (the office that deals with foreigners in each institution or province).

Similarly I have used:

*waiguoren* (more rudely *laowai*) the word for foreigner; *gweilo* is used in Hong Kong.

# Introduction

In July 1990 I retired from my career in education. Two years earlier I had been lucky enough to secure the promise of what proved to be an all-consuming role as GAP's first project manager for China, and, though I handed over the leading position to a valued colleague in 1995, I continued thus until 1999.

GAP Activity Projects Ltd. (GAP) is a non profit-making charity, founded in 1972, and now, over thirty years later, (2003) sends about 1,500 young people between school and university to 34 different countries worldwide. They are engaged mainly in TEFL work as assistants, but some – about 20% – do social work and another 10% are involved in conservation. In return, increasingly large numbers of overseas young people come on exchange to the UK each year. Though GAP is generously backed by some businesses and institutions, all volunteers have to pay their own travel and other expenses. In return, while working, they usually have free accommodation and food and some small sums of "pocket money" for incidentals. The China project, itself relatively recent and wholly concerned with language teaching, was first mooted in 1988, and after some negotiation started exchanging young people two years later. GAP's salaried staff in Reading is still small, and all other workers, project managers and interviewers, are voluntary.

My own real contact with China had begun in 1983, when my wife and I visited the country on a then usual group tour of the major Chinese cities; Beijing, Xi'an, Nanjing, Suzhou, Shanghai, Guilin and Guangzhou. But the scene in 1983, only seven years after Mao's death, was very different from now (2003) or indeed from when GAP started there (1990). Maoist dress was commonplace. The PLA were only just changing from their traditional baggy clothes to modern smart uniform. In the early 1980s there were still a few remaining elderly women with feet deformed from early foot binding. Massive steam locomotives still hauled passenger trains. Domestic passenger aircraft were usually noisy turbo-props; the smart, comfortable and ubiquitous Boeings and Airbuses were still in the future. All the cities were dusty and dimly lit in an effort to save energy – on our first night in China, I vividly remember stumbling through great crowds of students in Tiananmen Square who were sitting on the ground, enjoying the evening air, and whom I could hardly see. It was similar in Xi'an, Nanjing and Shanghai. Our hotels were not open to the Chinese. In one city a senior history academic, a professor, who furtively visited us in our hotel room would not let me show him out of the hotel for fear of being detected. Nevertheless Chinese everywhere were desperate to practise English, and, when we could, we left the tour group and engaged the local people in conversation. At the end of this journey, and another trip in 1987 (from Siberia and Mongolia), we had seen many superb buildings and some beautiful countryside, but overwhelmingly it was the Chinese people themselves that attracted us, and they still do. Hence my delight in being given the role to start the China project.

In 1988 China was still emerging from the turbulent decade of the Cultural Revolution (1966-76). It was only twelve years since Mao Zedong had died, only ten since Deng Xiaoping published his Four Modernisations which heralded the, at first slow, introduction of market economics (and the end of unadulterated centralised corporatism) – often known as Reform and Opening, and characterized as the Chinese equivalent of Gorbachev's Glasnost and Perestroika. The Tiananmen "incident" was still a year in the future, and the total collapse of the Soviet-system was yet to come. The 1990s for China was a period of startling change socially, politically and economically – especially in the years covered by this book, 1990-1995. Western inward investment into China increased remarkably. China's official outlook on the world changed, and the Chinese could more and more readily travel to the West. Educational exchange, rare in 1990, became more and more commonplace by 1995, and certainly by 1999. In 1988 few UK organisations promoted this interchange, apart from VSO for older people and Project Trust, GAP's friendly rival. Backed wholeheartedly by the UK Foreign Office and the British Council, to whom we owe so much, GAP was in the forefront of providing adolescents a structured programme in China. For me the decade's work with China was exhilarating, combining as it did, continued work with young people, constant negotiation in providing placements, co-ordination with colleagues in both China and the UK, and increasing contact and friendship with the Chinese themselves.

Remarkably in those first years the Chinese officials required no formal signatures. The Agreement made in Nanjing in January 1990 between Professor Chen Wenxiang and John Cornell, the GAP director, stated that there "was no need to sign any formal agreement to launch this project. Rather we would run it on the basis of mutual trust and a determination on both sides to provide an efficient service for our young volunteers. Therefore these notes, together with the Annexes, which were agreed point by point on the 19th January 1990, form the basis of the GAP/China Project". This was not a sign of casual, loose-ended negotiation, but in line, I later learnt, with the ancient Chinese way of doing business, much as our old London Stock Exchange used to operate on the adage "My word is my bond". In fact, the Chinese educationists, whether administrators or teachers, never let me down; they always fulfilled their obligations under our joint agreement to the full, in fact far more than the 100% required. It was only in the later part of the decade that Chinese bureaucratic procedures set in, and formal signatures and contracts were demanded. It was always a delight and a thrill to work with the Chinese, and to this day many remain my good friends.

* * *

None of this would have been possible without the generous support of so many people. Naturally I owe a very special debt of gratitude to John Cornell, the former director of GAP, who chose me, and in my absence set up the original agreement while I was still working. Throughout the years he has been a source of great strength; once the project was set up, though watchful, he never intruded into my running of the project. He was always appreciative, and gave support when needed; otherwise I was left to myself. In this way he had the knack of understanding how to make volunteers work willingly. The GAP House staff were always so supportive, especially my two registrars, Nicky and Lucille, who have both now left and married.

Outside the GAP organisation there are so many others who deserve thanks. In the UK the FCO has given great support; each year in Beijing successive ambassadors, Sir Alan Donald, Sir Robin McLaren, and Sir Leonard Appleyard, busy with so many other more important matters, each spared a full hour of their time – and sometimes hospitality – to listen to my report on how GAP was proceeding. There was no formal agenda, but a genuine interest in how our young people were doing. In addition, the consuls-general at Shanghai (and later at Guangzhou) gave much useful support and advice, in particular, Iain Orr, John Macdonald and Warren Townend. More closely involved with us were the directors of the British Council, Adrian Johnson (Beijing), Michael O'Sullivan, Duncan Jackman and Peter Grout in China and Tom Buchanan in Hong Kong. To Peter Grout I owe an especial debt of gratitude for welcoming ever-increasing numbers of GAPpers twice a year until 1993 at GAP's mandatory session in Shanghai. The Education Section of the Chinese Embassy in London were especially helpful and hospitable to our young volunteers before they left; we owe a special debt of gratitude to Professors Zhang Maizeng, Zheng Rongxuan and Zhang Taijing, and also to the staff of the Great Britain-China Centre, Belgrave Square, especially Nicola McBean, Anna Johnson, Laura Rivkin and Katie Lee.

I cannot speak too highly of the particularly fruitful and friendly relationship between the GAP-China project and Rolls Royce plc; I owe so much gratitude to the company, and especially to Richard Hill, then Manager of International Training, and his office, and to D'Arcy Payne, Corporate Director. They set up our placements in the four air colleges of CAAC, and provided back-up support on the ground in China from their staff, including Dr. Richard Thorne, especially at Baiyun Airport, Guangzhou, and at Tianjin. They also provided useful preliminary briefings in their Mickleover headquarters, Derby, for our volunteers. CAAC's own Director of Training in Beijing, Simon Yang Sheng Jun, was also helpful.

In China itself we owe much not only to the principals and staff of the schools and colleges, but also especially to the officials of each provincial Education Commission (*jiaowei*), amongst whom I will principally name those on whom I most relied and who became such good friends; Yu Shuigen and Du Jian in Zhejiang, Gao Yuemin and He Xingchu in Jiangsu, Qiu Bing and Zhang Jie Yuan in Fujian, Sui Zhi Qiang and Sun Hai Feng in Qingdao and Cai Li and Tan Jun in Sichuan. In Hong Kong likewise I thank Paul Chan for his friendship and hard work in extending and running the Hong Kong project in its early days. The Friends of GAP-China in Hong Kong; Sir Quo Wei Lee, David Tang, The Hon. Ronald Arculli, The Hon. Rosanna Wong, Simon Murray and David Gilkes, not only supported the project generously with resources but with their valuable time in giving me advice and ideas. I am grateful to them all.

The biggest debt of all I owe to the volunteers themselves who have done so much to make my GAP decade the most invigorating of my life. I owe much to Dan Large, a former GAPper at Li Shui, who has inspired me to commit my experiences to writing and has given me so much useful advice and support in the process; without him I would not have completed it. Above all, I thank my wife, Susan, who not only supported and sustained my activities over a decade, but has been an invaluable adviser in writing this work. She has had to endure much.

.

# 1. Genesis

Nineteen eighty-nine was a climactic year in China. In Beijing the Tiananmen "incident" shook Deng Xiao Ping's government, and there was considerable loss of face – the planned ceremonial welcome to the Soviet President Mikhail Gorbachev, due to take place in Tiananmen Square, had to be abandoned. The resulting repression of student and worker activism sent shivers around the world. Many wondered whether this brutish crackdown heralded a return to old xenophobia, to the Maoist excesses of the Cultural Revolution. Many wondered, too, if all the bridges, built since the days of "ping-pong" diplomacy and Nixon's historic meeting with Zhou En Lai in 1972, would be forgotten. Would Deng Xiao Ping's Four Modernisations of 1978 also be rescinded? The atmosphere was gloomy, even tense and unsteady. Some thought pessimistically that China, already possessing nuclear weapons and as enigmatic as ever, was a serious threat to the world.

Yet it was on the afternoon of 6th June 1989, before the dust had settled on the Tiananmen confrontation two days before, that John Cornell, Director of GAP, and I, Project Manager of its embryo China venture, rang at the door of the Chinese Embassy's Education Section. This building in West Ealing at 51 Drayton Green, was red-brick, gaunt, still bearing the redolence of a convent, which it once had been. Zhang Maizeng, First Secretary, and his wife Zheng Rongxuan, Second Secretary, welcomed us in. Aware of the strained sensitivity of our timing while cataclysmic events in China were still continuing, John and I had already planned our introductory remarks. We decided on something neutral. "We are sorry about what is happening in China." Zhang Maizeng at once blandly replied, "Yes, so are we. Let's talk about education." Zhang and his wife were a competent and affable couple, seconded from their work as professors of English at Nankai University, Tianjin. Zhang was a large man with a

1

great sense of humour, apparently easygoing, while Zheng, his wife, was neat, meticulous and thorough, and equally friendly. They immediately put us at our ease; with them at least, Tiananmen would not cast a shadow over our plans. They had already thoroughly prepared the ground for our discussion which started at once.

The story of the GAP-China Project really begins over a year earlier, early in 1988. In January, John Cornell, then the new Director of GAP, had written to schools appealing for retiring staff-members to consider working voluntarily for the organisation. I was to retire two years later, in 1990, and jumped at the idea, attracted by the prospect of combining continued work with young people and my interest in foreign cultures. In late January 1988 John replied, warmly summoning me for interview at Reading on Tuesday, 12th April. After meeting me at the rail-station, we walked to the temporary GAP offices then in King's Road. The rather dreary accommodation above a language school was not encouraging; it was noisy with traffic, pokey and cramped, hot and stuffy in summer.

John introduced me to a couple of the staff; Eric, a retired major, who was Finance Officer, and Shirley, the PA. But it was John who immediately impressed me. Recently retired from the army as a brigadier, his last job had been as defence adviser to the Indian Government, and, while in Delhi, his wife, Caroline, became involved in work with Tibetan refugees. Both were deeply committed to the Third World. A man with an obviously warm and deeply caring heart, he had the uncommon knack of making people want to work hard for no pay. The secret was to make GAP work enjoyable, and under him in spite of much hard work, it was fun. GAP became a family – most of us volunteer staff were of much the same age, between 60 and 70. Project managers' meetings, held quarterly, ran, without a lunch break, from 10 a.m. to 2.30 p.m., but always ended with an enjoyable buffet lunch. In the early days the GAP "family" had parties, to which we subscribed, and one of which in particular, I remember, was at

2

the London Zoo. John Cornell frequently showed special care for individual volunteers in trouble, or spouses, temporarily bereft of their project manager husbands or wives.

John instantly enthused me. I consequently agreed to work for GAP, but not fully until my retirement in July 1990, over two years later. When asked in which country I was interested in to work, I replied that I had been to China twice as a tourist since 1983, and was fascinated by it. As GAP apparently had nothing going there, John was immediately keen to offer it to me, once he had checked on my administrative experience. We agreed that, because I was not yet retired, we should share the work in setting up the project. On 6th June 1988 John wrote confirming my appointment as Project Manager. So my long eleven-year association with GAP and China began.

In spite of this little seemed to happen until March 1989, when John and I met others for lunch at the Dragon's Nest restaurant in Shaftesbury Avenue. Nicola McBean, Director of the Great Britain-China Centre, with her colleague, Anna Johnson, hosted the meal; other guests were Pan Wenguo, the Chinese Embassy's Counsellor (Education), and Zhang Maizeng, First Secretary. Here I saw for the first time John at his most persuasive, and his exposé of GAP organisation and philosophy clearly impressed the two Chinese. Zhang agreed to have all the GAP literature translated and transmitted to several provinces. Though he himself was a representative of the central government, Zhang advised us always to deal directly with provincial governments rather than negotiating through Beijing − advice later frequently repeated. To me it was fascinating that provincial governments had so much autonomy in what I thought was a highly centralised state. (Subsequently, I learnt from a sinologist friend that this was also the case under the Qing and earlier dynasties. Marxist centralisation under Mao Zedong was a temporary aberration.) We were delighted that all would be well. Before our next meeting later in the year the June events in Tiananmen Square were to cast doubts in our minds.

On 6th June we arrived at the Chinese Embassy, and had the meeting already described. Late that year, 1989, through the embassy's work we received positive responses from four provinces – Jiangsu, Zhejiang, Fujian and Guizhou. Guizhou we ruled out as too poor – and, so soon after Tiananmen, too remote for safety. Even in the other three, all maritime provinces, we felt it essential at that early stage for all volunteers to work near an airport from where, if necessary, they could be quickly airlifted out. Thus we posted the first three pairs to provincial capitals, in no way remote, and yet providing a sufficient challenge for our volunteers. Nevertheless we were still concerned that the FCO might discourage us. On 7th September, a Thursday, John and I visited the FCO to hear its views, but the Head of the China Desk, told us that, though officially cold towards the Chinese Government after Tiananmen, they were still keen for all bilateral contacts and exchanges, especially in the educational field, to continue and even to develop. That was good news.

All three of these provincial capitals, Nanjing (Jiangsu), Hangzhou (Zhejiang) and Fuzhou (Fujian), had been important in Chinese history. Nanjing was twice the national capital, once early in the Ming dynasty (1358-1644) and again under Chiang Kai Shek in the Guomintang period (1928-37 and 1945-49). It was here that the British forced Qing imperial officials to sign the Unequal Treaties (1842), ceding Hong Kong and forcing open the five original "treaty ports" to foreign trade. Later from 1853 to 1864 it was the capital of the Taiping rebellion, until it was captured with much slaughter by the Qing government with the aid of Britain and the United States. Then, when the Japanese invaded in 1937, the seven-week atrocity, known as the Rape of Nanjing, took place with the murder of over 60,000 Chinese. Hangzhou also has a long history and was, in 1200, the capital of the southern Song dynasty. Not only does it claim to be the original ambience of the silk industry, it had also prospered by its proximity to the sea and its position at one end of the seventh century Grand Canal, which connected it with the north.

Noting its fresh water canals, Marco Polo in the thirteenth century described it as one of the finest cities of the world; with its population then of well over 1.5 million it was arguably the biggest city in the world. Fuzhou from early times had been a significant trading centre, and was one of the original five treaty ports under the unequal Treaty of Nanjing (1842), the others being Shanghai, Guangzhou, Xiamen and Ningbo. In the 1990s it ranked second only to Xiamen as a city for Taiwanese investment.

As I was still working full time, it was John who planned the initial visit to the three provinces in January 1990. His Staff College training, his diplomatic skills, his persuasive powers also signalled him as the right person to go, especially in the tricky months after Tiananmen, and it was in Nanjing that the GAP-China agreement was made with the Chinese. Though it was sometimes called the Nanjing Agreement, I always studiously tried to avoid such a term, too unfortunately reminiscent of the infinitely more important Unequal Treaty of 1842! Meanwhile, the previous September 21st (1989) I made my first appearance as China Project Manager at the annual GAP Conference, held that year at Rugby School, where I announced our plans for China.

Employment at my school ended on July 1st 1990, and my full-time voluntary GAP commitment began. Already on May 25th, the Friday of half term, John and I had interviewed and chosen our first six volunteers for the three placements John had already negotiated, at Nanjing Foreign Language School, Hangzhou Foreign Language School and Fuzhou No.1 Middle School – a prestigious "key school", as the Chinese called their best middle schools. Interviewing took place in the same offices in King's Road where John had first interviewed me fifteen months before. It was half term, and the candidates were on the verge of 'A' level exams. I vividly remember the cramped rooms, the hot, stuffy atmosphere, and the traffic noise outside. We were late in the interviewing year. For Fuzhou we chose Christian Turner, a historian from Marlborough, and Simon Hughes, a future medical student from Guildford Grammar School; for Hangzhou, Keri Glenday from Millfield and Astra Holmes from Richmond College, and for Nanjing, Matthew Ball also from Millfield and Dan Hucker from Bristol Grammar School. On this memorable hot, steamy day we had netted the first six of many hundred future China GAPpers. The ambience in simplistic, makeshift GAP offices I later found duplicated in many education offices in the Chinese provinces; they were very different from the spruce, glitzy offices of Hong Kong I was soon to discover and the new Hong Kong look-alikes in Eastern China which came into being by the end of the decade.

Briefing day was set for August 28th 1990, in the Great Britain-China Centre. Our group consisted of the six volunteers, John, one or two parents and me, so small in number that we could sit round one small table in the Centre's library – unthinkable now with sixty GAPpers each time and at least as many parents. Nicola McBean gave us personal views on working in China. A reception followed at the Embassy's Education Section in Ealing, which became something of a tradition. It was a pleasant start.

On Wednesday, August 29th, we saw the volunteers off on their long flight by Pakistan Airlines to Beijing via Karachi. A few days later on September 6th at Gatwick, John, Maizeng, Rongxuan and I met the first Chinese teachers. The project was under way.

## 2. My first GAP visit (October – November 1990)

The time came for my first visit to the placements. There were only three of them, all in the provincial capitals, Fuzhou in Fujian, Nanjing in Jiangsu and Hangzhou in Zhejiang. In planning the trip I realised I must at some stage visit our ambassador in Beijing, Sir Alan Donald, and also establish relations with our consul-general in Shanghai, who had responsibility for welfare of all UK citizens in Jiangsu and Zhejiang provinces. On this first visit I decided to call on the ambassador at the end of the tour, to give him an up-to-date report on how GAP was getting started. I visited the Shanghai consulate-general at the beginning.

Apart from inspecting the placements already operating, I had a secondary plan – to cast GAP's net more widely and search for new placements beyond the three original provinces. My overall intention was then – and still was to the end of my term nine years later in 1999 – to keep the volunteers as far apart as reasonably possible. Groups of GAPpers congregating together in close proximity would, in my view, militate against the ultimate object of providing a real experience of self-reliance, independence and integration with the Chinese. I therefore built into my present schedule the two port-cities of Qingdao and Tianjin. Qingdao, still an important naval base and the fourth largest port in China, had before 1914 been a German concession area where the world-renowned German-type Tsingtao beer was, and still is, brewed. Bavarian style buildings remain. Tianjin, formerly known in the west as Tientsin, was historically the port for old Beijing at the junction of the Grand Canal from the south and the River Hai from the sea. In the nineteenth century, by the Treaty of Tianjin (1858) and a subsequent war, it was a concession port first of the British and French, and eventually after 1895 for other nations, including Austria-Hungary, Germany and Japan. Our old acquaintances, the "two professors", John's phrase for Zhang Maizeng and Zheng

7

Rongxuan, previously seconded to the London Embassy, were now back in their professorial posts at the prestigious Nankai University in Tianjin, known colloquially as Nanda. They were pressing us hard to put a placement in Tianjin, more specifically at the Foreign Language Institute.

My wife, Susan, accompanied me on this first occasion. She had enjoyed our tourist visits to China in 1983 and 1987, and now was keen to give me support and confidence in this new enterprise. It was for me a new world, and it was relatively soon after the Tiananmen "incident", a mere sixteen months before.

## Shanghai

We landed at Beijing early on October 21st, only to find that the tickets for the onward domestic flight to Shanghai, our first destination, had not been booked. In those days it was still impossible outside China to book internal flights, and the agent in Beijing appeared not to have already done so. In 1990 individual travel was still hazardous and complicated, and at the old Beijing Airport there was turmoil in getting a booking. Our agent eventually met us, charged an iniquitous 250 yuan for her service, bought the tickets, and we were soon on a comfortable 280 seater DC bound for Shanghai. When we landed at Shanghai Hongqiao Airport, the initial sensation was depressing. The terminal then was old and decrepit, and there was a phenomenal crowd trying to get the few taxis available. Eventually, however, we reached the Heping Fandian (Peace Hotel), originally named the Cathay, and built by Victor Sassoon in the 1920s. Here it was good to be installed in a spacious suite. We enjoyed a turn on the Bund before collapsing into bed.

Our stay in Shanghai was brief. It included a visit to Iain Orr, the British Consul-General, who was helpful in giving advice. He took us for lunch to the newly constructed Mandarin Hotel, where we met a couple from our Beijing Embassy, and discussed the Tiananmen affair. In the afternoon we visited the British Council, and met the Director, Duncan Jackman. All these were fruitful contacts. The day ended with a supper with Gu Ping, an old friend of ours from 1983, now a lecturer at the Conservatory of Music.

Iain Orr, the Consul-General, keen to help find placements for GAP, the next day took us to No. 3 Girls' School which he knew. This was a prestigious establishment, built by Methodist missionaries in 1892, and counted amongst its early 20th century pupils the Soong sisters, who married Sun Yat Sen and Chiang Kai Shek (in Mandarin Jiang Jie Shi). It still had a high standard. We met the principal, Mr. Chen Bing Fu, and his colleagues, with whom I discussed GAP and its possible involvement here. They were certainly intrigued by the idea, and I hoped to follow up the prospect, but I was later to discover from our Chinese GAP co-coordinators in Hangzhou that my visit had been a monumental blunder. We put proposals to the school without permission from the Shanghai City Education Commission. I was, for a time, persona non grata, and quickly learnt a lesson in protocol.

**Fuzhou**

And so, having battled through the crowds of Japanese tourists at Shanghai Airport, pushing and shoving their way around us as we made our way to the plane, we flew to Fuzhou. The flight was short − one hour − and comfortable. At the old Fuzhou Airport, diminutive, rather primitive and homespun compared with the present one, we had a magnificent welcome from the two volunteers, Simon Hughes and Christian Turner, who turned up with Zhu Ding Feng, the headmaster of No. 1 School, and Qiu Bin, the GAP agent, a member of the Fujian *jiaowei* (The Chinese usefully abbreviate the Mandarin for Education Commission to *jiaowei*. From now onwards for brevity's sake I shall use this expression.) After settling into the Dong Hu (East Lake) Hotel, we were taken to see the Gu Shan, the Drum Mountain, and its ancient Yongquan monastery, over a 1,000 years old. In the evening we were guests at an exotic banquet, given by the Director of the *jiaowei*, Ye Pinqiao. This was my first experience of such an occasion with its many colourful, diverse dishes, beer, wine and baijiu; it was also my first experience of the sensibly abrupt ending of these events. At 8 p.m. the director suddenly rose and said goodbye. That was the end.

My visit the next morning to Fuzhou No. 1 Middle School was my first to any GAP placement, the first of so many. The school was academically excellent and large with 2,000 pupils and 23 teachers of English. Reportedly, seven of its former students were then members of the Chinese Institute of Science. After welcoming us at 8 a.m. the headmaster showed us round. We were first shown the labs. In Simon's view the standard in Maths and Chemistry in the senior classes was at least up to sixth form standard at his own school, Guildford Grammar. Equipment too was good. There were 52 computers in the computer room which for 1990 anywhere was high. (I soon learnt that dense, detailed statistics were an important part of any description of, or "introduction" to, an institution.) The school also had its own private radio station. These turned out to be gifts from former students now of the Fujian diaspora, now living in Taiwan and elsewhere overseas. They were soon to have a new stadium and large concert hall paid for by Taiwan. When I remonstrated that surely these were Guomintang members, the headmaster merely said, "Forget the politics. We are here for education."

I then attended my first-ever GAP class. With incredible vigour Chris was teaching Junior 2 (13 year olds) about plane journeys, about going by taxi and by bus. The classroom door turned out to represent London − "Not 'Lurndurn', but 'London'," as Chris got the class to repeat several times. Then we moved on to Simon's Senior 2 class (equivalent of lower sixth); he told them a complicated story about a princess, and their test was to disentangle reversed sentences. Simon, a potential doctor, now an anaesthetist, had all the makings of a competent teacher. We visited the GAPpers' accommodation, for which the *jiaowei* had found special money to provide

10

what the GAP agreement specified. They had their own front door and washing facilities, a sitting room and two bedrooms. They were paid 400 yuan (Y400) a month which compared favourably with the ordinary teacher's Y300, and they taught twenty periods a week, while most teachers did twelve. The volunteers, however, appreciated the latter had massive marking to do for classes of sixty.

After another elaborate banquet, this time at lunch, hosted by the Director of the Fujian Trade Commission, Mr. Wang Qu, we were taken to see No. 3 Middle School, where our February volunteers were destined to go. This school, near the West Lake, was in a much pleasanter ambience than No. 1. The deputy headmaster, Mr. Xie Yong Quan, a jovial man, gave us a great welcome, and at the gate, much to our surprise, the school greeted us with a large notice saying "Welcome Dr. and Mrs. Marshall to our school". We discussed GAP in the impressive conference room decked in flowers, a mass of them along the centre of the floor, and inspected the proposed accommodation, still being converted to the GAP norm. We returned to the hotel, where we had a good chat with Simon and Chris, the first of many such discussions through the years. They were a fine couple, exemplary ambassadors for GAP, for the UK and for themselves. It says much about the parlous situation in Fuzhou in 1990 that they were unable to buy batteries; we handed over some of ours.

On our last morning in Fuzhou we visited the white jade Buddha temple, and West Lake Park, that day crowded with old people for it was apparently "Respect for the Elderly" day (October 26th) – a day suitable for myself. After lunch we departed for the little airport, still primitive enough not to have electronic luggage surveillance, and all baggage had to be opened for inspection before being taken on board. A tedious procedure, so very different from the new Fuzhou Airport only a few years later.

11

## Nanjing

After a two-hour vibrantly noisy flight in a small 60-seater turbo-prop plane, we landed at Nanjing, where we were met by the Jiangsu GAP agent, Gao Yuemin, a smiling, jolly person who was to become a great friend. With him were the two Nanjing GAPpers, Matthew Ball and Dan Hucker. We were immediately installed in the Shuangmen (Double Gate) Hotel, an old building, constructed perhaps in the 1920s. In front was the former British Embassy of the Guomintang period, when Nanjing was the Chinese capital. It is a typical British old colonial-style building of the 20s and 30s. We hardly had time to settle in, when we were whisked off to yet another banquet, this time hosted by the Vice-Director of the Jiangsu Education Commission, Mr. Ye Chun Sheng, who declared himself strongly in favour of the GAP project. Also present was Zhang Xing Hua, Director of Foreign Affairs, whom I came to know well over the years. So keen was he on Jiangsu province's twinning with Essex County, that whenever I arrived, he always proudly wore an Essex tie. The food was excellent but with less emphasis on seafood than at Fuzhou.

Our visit the next morning to the Nanjing Foreign Language School, prestigious throughout China, coincided with its Sports Day, and there was no teaching, so we met initially in the Foreign Experts' compound, imaginatively called "Dawn Garden", and then watched some sports. For the benefit of photographers I put the shot, not a skill of mine. After lunch in a nearby hotel, we returned to the school for a discussion with Mr. Dong Zheng Jing, the vice-principal, who had studied at the Polytechnic of Central London in 1985/6. He now analysed in meticulous detail the work of the two GAPpers, emphasising their need for more preparation in teaching method before arrival in China. I had a satisfactory chat with Matthew, but my planned discussion with Dan was abruptly − at the time I felt officiously − cut short when Mr. Xu Fachang, the Foreign Affairs Officer, brusquely ordered

12

us out to the sports; I had to content myself with talking to Dan on the sports field. All seemed to be going well with the couple, though they expressed some frustration at being cocooned in the foreigners' compound, the Dawn Garden, where they were allowed no contact with the students out of class hours. Nevertheless, as Dan admitted, they could indeed meet and talk with other Chinese, if, despite all the school's restrictive regulations, they went out into the city to search for them. Susan and I actually participated in the sports, much to the amusement of the students and hilarious for ourselves; we took part in the teachers' "race for the middle-aged", for which we apparently qualified; by running as a couple, awkwardly balancing a pole over a shoulder each.

Subsequently, Gao Yuemin, the Jiangsu GAP agent, took us to the magnificent Sun Yat Sen mausoleum, a fantastic experience in the evening light – a visit I was to repeat on several occasions in future years. A sumptuous banquet followed in the Dawn Garden, presided over by the three vice-presidents. Here we had fresh water crabs which they earnestly informed us were a special delicacy costing 35 yuan a pound, compared with pork at a mere five yuan. Dong was very friendly, and presented us with books and tapes to help our Chinese language studies.

On our last day in Nanjing a couple of students took us sightseeing in the morning, and we rounded the day off with an informal meal in a small Chinese restaurant with Matthew, Dan and a German student at the cost of a mere 37 yuan for the five of us, including beer. This was my first experience of these restaurants, which I used to patronise frequently in the years that followed.

**Hangzhou**

Seen off by Gao and Xu, we left on Monday, October 29th, by the 9.12 a.m. train for Hangzhou. It was a long, hot journey. Much of the time we were engaged in wearisome, lengthy conversations with a delegation of voluble, incessantly chattering Frenchmen; they were apparently electrical engineers. When at 6.15 p.m. we reached Hangzhou it was already dark. Met by the province's GAP agent, Yu Shuigen, and a Mr. Mao, vice-principal of the Hangzhou Foreign Language School, we were taken by minibus to our next abode, the Zhejiang Guest House. This was a complex of buildings in a beautiful setting, but rather a long way from the city centre. The main house was apparently Lin Biao's hideout before his air crash in September 1971. Our rather dreary room in No. 3 Building was typical of government accommodation, used for party conferences. We realised how lucky we were to have had better accommodation in Fuzhou and Nanjing. We retired early to bed.

Our first day in Zhejiang was mildly frustrating. Instead of seeing our GAPpers or their place of work, our immediate diet was, as so often, sightseeing and leisure, this time with Vice-Principal Mao and a Ms. Wan. After seeing the Lingjing Temple, then being returned to full religious use, we had a prolonged boat trip on the West Lake, the Xi Hu. Pleasant as this was, we wanted to hear how the GAP girls were faring, but for some reason that subject was at all times studiously avoided. Our frustrations grew in intensity. Eventually, however, in the late afternoon at long last we were taken to see the new Foreign Language School, still under construction. Here the principal, a delightful man, a scholar of Chinese literature, hosted yet another exotic meal, with Shaoxing wine from nearby. After dinner, 24 hours after our arrival in Hangzhou, we had what we were waiting for. We visited a class doing prep and I talked to one or two of the students. It happened to be the class normally taught by He Hong, our Chinese volunteer, then teaching in Beaconsfield. They clearly liked her, and had the charming idea of writing a card with their names on for me to take back to her. Our first day in Hangzhou, apart from the evening, was still ominous; there was little discussion about the GAPpers.

Nevertheless on Wednesday, I at last saw Keri Glenday in action. They clearly thought highly of her, for they had assigned her to the Institute of Financial Management where

14

her class comprised high-calibre trainee merchant bankers between the ages on 24 and 37. A Mandarin speaker herself – she had lived in Taiwan – and a former head girl of her school, she was coping most competently with this class of highly intelligent, mature students, who probed her with complex questions about the exact meaning and nuances of "features", "characteristics" and "personality". It was a bravura performance. I then visited Astra's class at the Foreign Language School. She had a difficult assignment with a group of rather unintelligent trainee waiters. It was hard for her.

**Hangzhou Conference**

On October 31st in the Foreign Language School, we held the first-ever annual conference of GAP agents in China. I chaired the meeting jointly with Professor Chen Wenxiang, our GAP senior co-coordinator, who at that time was vice-director of the Zhejiang Provincial Education Commission. Recently widowed, he was a remarkable character. Quietly spoken, yet with great charisma, he never failed to meet me with a smiling face and eyes, and one could each time feel the warmth of his personality. Always dressed impeccably in a neat Maoist suit, he made an immediate impact on me, and we at once forged a great relationship, though all our conversation had to be through interpreters. After a further two years as vice-director of the *jiaowei* he went back to academic life, to his former post as president of Zhejiang Agricultural University.

The GAP agents gathered for the meeting, Gao Yuemin from Nanjing, Zhang Jie Yuan, deputising for Qiu Bin, from Fuzhou, and Yu Shuigen, already here in Hangzhou. As Yu Shuigen was unable to attend for the full time – he had to deal with an Australian delegation – he was, for part of the conference, represented by a young, newly appointed official of the *jiaowei*, Du Jian, who then sported an English name, George, which we soon forgot to use. From then on we have always known him by his Chinese name, Du Jian. Yu Shuigen, with his director, Xu Yaogen, was over the years,

15

the true creative thinker of GAP-China strategy, but from that small beginning Du Jian became a key member of our team and, in fact, the real pivot of GAP-China for over a decade, upon whom we came to rely on for so much. We owe him and Yu Shuigen a remarkable debt of gratitude. The meeting, the first of many, held annually, went well. Far from being difficult, which I had feared, it demonstrated how friendly and supportive of GAP the Chinese were.

## The journey to Qingdao

My work in the three original provinces was now complete, and it was time to move on to the second phase of the journey, the search for new placements elsewhere. We set out for Qingdao and Tianjin. We left Zhejiang Guesthouse early the next morning, Thursday, November 1st, at 6.30 a.m. After wrestling with the Hangzhou rush hour, the driver reached the station in time for the 7.50 a.m. train for Shanghai. For this four-hour journey only hard seats were available, but this was not a problem. The carriage was hot; I noticed across the aisle a Hangzhou man learning Cantonese by tapes and discussion with his travelling companion, while outside were the endless rice fields and much agricultural activity. Yu Shuigen was also travelling in a different part of the train, and laden with books on his way to the FCO Chevening scholarship exam at the British Council. We reached Shanghai at about noon. After lunching at the Peace Hotel, we departed for Shanghai Hongqiao Airport to catch the advertised 5.30 p.m. flight to Qingdao. After a delay of two hours, caused, we were told, by mechanical problems, we took off at approximately 7.30 p.m. in a smart new plane.

## Qingdao

When we arrived in Qingdao at 9.15 p.m. it was already dark. At the airport, as we alighted from the aircraft, we noticed at once the cold bracing northern air, a great contrast from Shanghai. A young education official, Sun Hai Feng, who was to become a great friend, met us, and took us to our hotel, The

16

Huang Hai, where we met his boss, Sui Zhi Qiang. As we had arrived too late for hotel supper, we contented ourselves with a bowl of noodles to keep us going until the morning. The Huang Hai Hotel was new with a superb, startling view overlooking the bay.

In the hotel conference room the following morning we met Sui and Sun again, with a Mr. Wan Nienwen, the warm, good-humoured Dean of English from No. 9 School and an English teacher who acted as interpreter. I outlined GAP's philosophy and proposals for two hours, after which, while the school discussed the programme, Sun took us to Shan Qing Road "key" Primary School, impressively kitted out with a state of the art language lab. This was quite a revelation. As we entered a classroom the class of 40 to 50 eight year olds stood up and gave us a beautifully rehearsed and impressive welcome in splendid English. After this we toured a computer class, the new buildings and a new sports hall under construction. This was most striking; clearly Qingdao City was investing heavily in education.

After lunch at the hotel we walked down to the beach and watched hardy swimmers enjoying a lunch hour in the surf. As the only foreigners there, we were as usual an object of curiosity; a group of children gathered round excitedly to practise English. Sun Hai Feng arrived to take us to No. 9 School, the school we had discussed at the morning meeting in the hotel. This was a former German missionary school founded in 1900 by the scholarly sinologist, Richard Wilhelm, who later published his translation of the *Tao Te Ching* in 1910 and with a commentary in 1925. When we visited, it still had several superb old German half-timbered buildings, sadly in the process of demolition to make way for the new, ubiquitous concrete edifices so beloved by modern Chinese educationists. To my astonishment (I was more astonished in 1990 by this than later) we were there at a special time − to celebrate the 90th anniversary of Wilhelm's foundation of the school. We were taken to a room where there was an extensive exhibition of photographs of early German

17

missionary teachers and Chinese pupils and other memorabilia of those early years. It was a fascinating, intensely interesting display. The school was clearly proud of its missionary origins. Here we were in communist China witnessing a school's celebration of its foundation by a European Christian missionary. Paradoxes in modern China never cease to amaze one.

There followed yet another banquet in the Teacher's Guesthouse, hosted by the education commission's deputy director, Wang Xixian; together with No. 9's headmaster, Wan; Sui and Sun were also there. The food, this time prepared by some cookery students, was again splendid; one very beautiful dish, I remember, was made of slices of egg and other foods, built into the appearance of a peacock. There was a full range of drinks which in Qingdao I soon learnt was normal – Qingdao beer, red wine and maotai. It was a very relaxed, convivial evening. Afterwards Sun Hai Feng took us back to the Huang Hai where we spent an enjoyable hour and a half discussing his early life. He is a delightful person. His father was born on July 13th 1930, only eleven days before me. He joined the PLA in 1945, fought the Japanese, then the Guomintang and was then in the Korean War. How strange this was. Had I not been demobilised from National Service in 1950, his father and I might have been on opposite sides, perhaps facing one another in Korea. At the end of that war there was a shortage of Chinese naval officers, so he transferred to the navy, eventually becoming a senior officer at Qingdao's naval base. Sun's mother had been an army doctor in Korea, and Sun himself was born just north of the Korean border. One of his two older sisters was now a naval doctor. After much talk Sun left at 9.30 p.m. to do overnight security duty at the *jiaowei*.

On the Saturday, Sun Hai Feng gave us a sightseeing tour of the city. We visited the house, known as Huashilon, where Chiang Kaishek – Jiang Jie Shi in Putonghua – stayed in 1947, not long before his departure for Taiwan. This Bavarian-style building, formerly the German governor's residence, has a commanding, beautiful position overlooking the bay. As the three of us walked among the rocky pools, watching crabs and seeing people digging for worms, the bracing sea air reminded me so much of our native Suffolk coast, so refreshing after the murky, hot Chinese cities we had so far experienced. The Xia Yu Shan (Little Fish Hill), a delightful spot with Chinese style roofs, and then the pier built in wood by the Germans in about 1900, but later replaced in concrete, were other reminders of North Sea coasts. Here for the first time we experienced the bitter cold of winter.

After seeing the outside of the massive, stunning twin-spired German Catholic basilica where Sun says he goes at Christmas, and another onion-spired church, both so typically German, we met again in our hotel for another discussion. The *jiaowei* and the school declared a definite interest in GAP, but before making a final decision they had to await the translation of the GAP agreement to arrive from Yu Shuigen, our Chinese co-ordinator in Hangzhou. I was delighted, for this would be an excellent placement, if only they agreed. My first attempt to spread the project beyond the three core provinces seemed likely to succeed.

After another hour's chat at the hotel with Sun – apart from English he was also learning German and Japanese! – we left for the remarkable half-timbered station, also Bavarian in style, and boarded the 9.50 p.m. train (eventual destination Shenyang) for the 13-hour overnight rail journey for Tianjin. Our carriage companions were two Chinese senior engineers from Tianjin.

## Tianjin

It was Sunday, November 4th, when we woke to a dreary, misty day with the sun a dull orange disc struggling to break through, and the landscape flat with many neat, newly-built brick buildings. We arrived at Tianjin Xi (West) at 10.50 a.m., dead on time. As we dismounted, I heard my name called out. It was Maizeng, who with his wife, Rongxuan, had come to meet us. It was a world away from West Ealing, where we had last met. We were soon in a foreign expert's flat in the Foreign Language Institute. The accommodation, though a bit gloomy and dilapidated, was large, self-contained, and had its own sitting room. Gao arrived soon afterwards from Nanjing to help me with negotiations. It was excellent to have Gao's help. Though I introduced GAP myself in English at all later negotiations with new provinces, I also had a GAP agent, already well versed in GAP's ways, to vouch for us to his fellow-Chinese.

After a 12.00 lunch we met the vice-president and her staff, though it was Sunday, the one day free. Sitting bolt upright on a dais in the large conference hall with us all seated round the walls, she seemed to me, inexperienced with China, dauntingly regal and rather severe − a Queen Victoria figure. Her interpreter, probably more nervous than I, and whose English was certainly far from fluent, made matters worse by insisting I spoke more slowly, "it is such an important meeting." The truth was that he was unable to cope and soon Gao, skilfully competent in simultaneous translation, mercifully took over. A subsequent inspection of possible accommodation for GAPpers disappointingly revealed that, though the Institute was tertiary, it was less suitable than what we had already achieved by agreement, especially in Fuzhou. As we walked round the campus, the Dean of English asked if I knew of any retired teachers who would come instead of the GAPpers. I said I would see what I could find, but as a retired history teacher, I was of no use. He immediately suggested I should come myself. I was startled. Until that moment I had not realised I was at all marketable. The thought indeed plagued my mind for the next two or three years, and indeed later, I seriously thought of a year teaching in Zhejiang, but sadly it never materialized.

It was Monday when we visited the Foreign Language Middle School, parallel to those in Nanjing and Hangzhou. I had a good chat with 17 year olds, including one, who showed great interest in History and whose unusual English name was "Lincoln". When asked about History teaching methods in the

UK, I surprised them by saying that at their level we based our teaching on group discussion, an idea novel for them, for they still learned facts without debate. One girl asked me what happened in 1517! Why? Was she thinking of Luther's Ninety Five Theses or something Chinese?

The atmosphere was good, but again the accommodation was unsatisfactory. Whereas in the Institute they would have had to live in a foreign experts' compound, as in Nanjing, here in the language school there was nothing suitable – and the authorities were not prepared to modify what they had, as their opposite numbers had done so well in Fujian, and were doing in Zhejiang. Consequently, in my own mind I decided to rule Tianjin out – at least for the moment, despite the disappointment this might cause to our friends, the "two professors".

It was a bitter cold day, and for the first time we had to wear thick anoraks continuously, even in the conference room, where there was no heating until mid-November. After an afternoon of sightseeing we had a second formal meeting at the Institute, at which I explained my reservations. The President herself offered me a job, much to my surprise – they had watched how I got on with their senior students. I had to refuse again. Later that evening, after another generous banquet, Gao and I had a chat. He cautioned me of the danger of hurting Tianjin's feelings – in particular those of Maizeng and Rongxuan – if I went ahead with Qingdao and not Tianjin, but I was not worried. I could easily make the obviously valid excuse that at this early stage for GAP-China, and so soon after Tiananmen, Tianjin was too far away from the core provinces, much further than Qingdao. We agreed that in any case Tianjin had less to offer GAPpers than Fuzhou, Hangzhou and Nanjing. And so off to bed, or so we thought. At the room we found our loo overflowing all over the bathroom! I went and told Gao who kindly said he would leave his loo door open all night for us! We complimented each other on our sense of humour.

21

# To Beijing

That was our last day in Tianjin, for on Tuesday, November 6th, we left at 10.38 a.m. by the fast train for Beijing. Arriving on time nearly two hours later, we were soon in No. 2 building of the You Yi Binguan (Friendship Guesthouse). This was the first of many visits over the years to the gargantuan Russian-built hotel. In those days a good room could be had for a mere 130 yuan a night. Here we spent two days, during which Sir Alan Donald, the British Ambassador, and his wife, invited us to a formal lunch with ten others, mostly members of his staff, either diplomatic or British council officials. This was an excellent occasion. The food was good, and we were again using knives and forks, which seemed strangely awkward and heavy after weeks with only chopsticks. It was helpful to be able to report on GAP's progress. Not only was Sir Alan most supportive, listening attentively to my report and promising to keep a watchful eye over developments, but it was also useful to meet so many who would be useful contacts in GAP's future in China. The rest of our time in Beijing, apart from meeting my VSO opposite number, Tina Redshaw, was spent less importantly in sightseeing those places we had not visited in 1983 and 1987 − the Summer Palace, so peaceful on a November evening, and on the following day, out to the Fragrant Hills.

We left by Dragon Air for Hong Kong on Friday, November 9th. I remember vividly the extreme cold of Beijing Airport's departure lounge − it was too early in November for public heating. Hong Kong, where we spent a few days, was a welcome and memorable contrast, the sun, the brightness and the welcome warmth. We attended the Remembrance Day ceremonies at the Cenotaph in Chater Square, the same ritual, the same music as in Whitehall, but there was sun, white naval uniforms and the Governor, also clad in white with a plumed hat, in astonishing contrast with the murkiness, and the heavy grey and black uniforms and suits of Whitehall.

We flew home on November 13th, a Tuesday. An incident, while we were waiting for the flight in a hotel lounge gave me another abiding memory. A waitress served us coffee. She spoke such good English, unlike her Hong Kong Cantonese-speaking colleagues. We asked her her name and where she was from. She was "Wan Shi Li (Lily) from Xinjiang in the far North West," she whispered. "My colleagues say that I speak such bad English, and am only a poor peasant." We were able to assure her that her English was far, far better, and certainly we were impressed by her manner. This conversation at the end of our trip gave me a vision of the future. How different were the mainland Chinese from those in Hong Kong, and how much clearer their spoken English. I felt heartened for the future of GAP in China. The flight home too was memorable for the unusual emptiness of the plane. Our jumbo airliner had a mere 85 passengers on board. It was the middle of the Gulf War and we had to put down twice in the Gulf − at Dubai and Bahrain − to change crew.

# 3: 1991-1992 Years of Expansion – Guangzhou, Qingdao, Shanghai and Hunan

## The 1991 (May and October) Prelude

Nineteen-ninety-two was a year of major expansion westwards into Central China, but preparations for this had been laid beforehand in the year before. In January 1991, a mere two months after my first GAP visit to China and Hong Kong, I had been to the latter again for a brief five days. This was for a fundraising drive, but perhaps more importantly it proved to be the seed of the Hong Kong Project (see chapter 7).

## May 1991

In May that year, at the start of my China visit, I was in Hong Kong again to look at possible placements for the new Hong Kong project, and to make a brief day-visit to Guangzhou to negotiate the placement at the CAAC's Civil Aviation Academy (see chapter 6). After this I flew to both Hangzhou and Qingdao. In Hangzhou the Foreign Language School had proved unsatisfactory, and we had to look for a replacement. Early on the morning of May 28th, Yu Shuigen and Du Jian took me to the Zhejiang Institute of Technology (ZIT), which at first sight looked reasonable; and certainly the accommodation was what we wanted. I decided to agree to it. Then all three of us took a two-hour drive to Shaoxing, a traditional small town with a population of 200,000, and reportedly Zhou En Lai's family seat, a delightful place with a fine pagoda and other old buildings. Shaoxing is famous for its rice wine, produced for the imperial table in ancient times and still for the Communist leadership in Beijing. I was able to see the 2000 years old, genuinely ancient temple, reportedly saved from the Red Guards through Zhou En Lai's personal intervention. The director of the city's *jiaowei* gave us an enjoyable lunch, and the famous Shaoxing rice wine flowed freely.

24

They took me to see the teachers' college, where the accommodation and the ambience all looked good – good enough, with the work to be done, to make an excellent placement. This was our first attempt at a teachers' college. These institutions trained teachers for the junior three years of middle schools (teachers' [or normal] universities training those for the senior three years). It was Yu Shuigen's perceptive idea to try these, and it became a model for our future development, not only within Zhejiang province but elsewhere, in the west, in Hunan, Sichuan and Yunnan. He was offering an extra Zhejiang placement for part of a year, for which I was to accept one more Chinese volunteer annually, making three in all from the province. We agreed therefore that in 1991-1992 we should have two Zhejiang placements, one at the Zhejiang Institute of Technology (ZIT) from September, and a second at Shaoxing in alternate semesters from February 1992.

From Hangzhou I moved on to Qingdao for only a brief stay this time to make final arrangements for the first GAPpers to go in September 1991 to No. 9 School, now being designated a fully-fledged Foreign Language School. I stayed in the Dongfang Hotel near the centre of the city. From there I flew home.

## October 1991

The following October I was in the Far East again, amazingly for the third time within a year, this time for my annual round of inspecting placements, but I had a second purpose. I was determined to pursue speedily my original aim of spreading GAP's placements inland far beyond the coastal provinces. After calling on the new ambassador, Sir Robin Maclaren, in Beijing – he kindly gave me an hour of his time – I flew on to Qingdao to see all was satisfactory with the first volunteers there; Dan Croft and Stephen Park. They had eventually settled well in spite of some early administrative problems. Though their accommodation, cramped in one room in the Espero, a practice hotel for the No. 29 (Tourism) School was

25

not good, I was confident that Qingdao would be a first-rate placement.

After travelling by train to Nanjing where, despite the Dawn Garden problem, noted in the last chapter, all seemed well with the GAPpers, Rosemary Beale and Emma Hunt, I travelled on to Shanghai to visit the consulate, where the Consul-General, John MacDonald, gave me lunch. While staying at the Peace Hotel, I received a summons from Li Shou Pao, a leader of the YMCA; in fact, he turned out to be not only its National General Secretary, and a senior member of the Shanghai city government, but also a vice-chairman on the Three Self Movement, the Chinese non-Catholic amalgamation of churches. He sent a car for me and we had a chat at his headquarters, during which he asked me, almost upbraided me, as to why I had no placement in Shanghai with all its British historical connections. Naturally as usual I was reticent, almost coy, about British involvement in the city over the past 150 years, "Not very favourable connections," I said. He disagreed, saying I should try. He was clearly keen, but, as there was no time to follow it up at that point, I had to leave it at that. At this stage we still had no one in Shanghai, and I was sad at that.

Two days later I was in Hangzhou from where I made a second visit to Shaoxing Teachers' College, our new placement in Zhejiang, away from any provincial capital, where the first GAPpers, Jane Alexander and Andrea Ledward, had not yet arrived, but were due to go the following January, 1992. I noted with gratitude that the principal had fulfilled my accommodation requests to the letter. Shaoxing, as a teachers' college, was a great advance, as we have noted; it turned out to be a model for development within the province and for elsewhere. Thus this was a significant step. When I visited the Zhejiang Institute of Technology, on the other hand, I could see that it was proving unsatisfactory, indeed little short of disastrous. The two volunteers, Adrian Tucker and Zaid Al Zaidy, were not given enough work to do, felt isolated and the food was poor, so we decided to terminate the arrangement with effect from June 1992.

In Hangzhou, Du Jian was now GAP agent in Zhejiang, while Yu Shuigen was away on his Chevening Scholarship at Sussex University in the UK. Du Jian and I now made our first significant reconnaissance into Central China — to Hunan province. We were, in any case, due to visit Fuzhou together for the 1991 annual GAP conference on Saturday, November 2nd, but en route we made a circuitous tour to visit the Hunan provincial *jiaowei* on the way. It was for both of us the first visit to that part of China. We flew to Changsha, the provincial capital, on Thursday, October 31st, where we were met by a young official, Li Shihong. The next morning we had a fascinating sightseeing tour of Changsha, its ancient university, originally the Yuelu Academy, dating from the Song dynasty and reputedly the second oldest in the world after Cairo. Mao Zedong had studied there, which gave it added kudos. We also visited Orange Island (Juzizhou) where, as a student, he reportedly used to write poems. Interesting though all this was, our time was limited and we needed to get down to negotiation as soon as possible. Once again our hosts misunderstood our mission. We had come here to discuss GAP and also see at least one middle school or a college, not to see the sights. Eventually after protest they gave us a swift, rather unsatisfactory glance at a middle school and we had a short talk with Shu Fanqing, the head of the *waiban* at the *jiaowei*. The discussion was only brief, too brief. Shu discouragingly murmured that they already had VSO volunteers, but nevertheless undertook to report to his colleagues, and, if all seemed satisfactory, he would arrange for a more extended meeting and visit in 1992, when we could see a college.

That evening Du Jian and I wandered around the shopping area. He was surprised to find here that prices surprisingly were 50% higher than in Hangzhou, an interesting fact; presumably in the inland city there were fewer market forces operating. Or were transport costs a factor? Hunan was as strange and new to him as it was to me. In fact, in one shop, when speaking in Mandarin, he tried to buy an item. The shop assistant would only answer in English, which mystified us both, until we realised she could not understand Du Jian's Zhejiang accent. Coupling that with the fact that he was accompanying me, a foreigner, a *waiguoren* or *laowai*, she must have thought Du Jian an overseas Chinese. He remonstrated "Here I am in my own country, speaking my own language and I can't be understood!" This became a standing joke between us in the years ahead.

Du Jian and I flew on to Fuzhou for the 1991 GAP conference on November 5th. Professor Zhang Xiangwan, director of the Jiangsu *jiaowei*, had flown specially from Nanjing for two nights for the occasion. This was a remarkable kindness, for he had great responsibility in Jiangsu as director of education for the whole of Jiangsu province with its 71 million people, larger than the whole of the UK. The conference in the morning lasted four hours and went well, despite my having to raise the thorny problem over Chinese volunteers' return airfares to the UK – which some Chinese schools demanded they should refund. In the afternoon I spent time with the two Fuzhou GAPpers, Peter Price-Thomas and Iain Pocock, a delightful, competent and dedicated couple. That night for the first and only time I presided at a special fully formal Chinese banquet with a multitude of small dishes of delicacies; these two directors of Jiangsu and Fujian (a population of 31 million) sat on my right and on my left. Two days later I flew to Guangzhou to visit our first volunteers there, Pippa Keggin and Amy Walker. I watched them teaching English not to engineering students, but lecturers, and doing it efficiently. The accommodation was good; they had even chosen their floor tiles. I then flew to Hong Kong and then home.

By the end of that year, 1991, GAP's development in the first four maritime provinces and in CAAC's Air China Aviation Academy at Guangzhou was, on the whole, with the one exception of Zhejiang Institute of Technology, running smoothly. The Hong Kong project had also got under way, for in January 1992 the first two Hong Kong volunteers, Archie Hawken and Brett Perkins, went out to start the embryo project there (see chapter 7). Our sortie into Hunan in November had not yet borne fruit, so it was now time to make a firmer move into the mainland interior. My normal annual regime had now fallen into place. In the autumn I would make a comprehensive inspection of all existing placements to see how the GAPpers were and to solve problems, where necessary, while the spring and early summer tour I reserved for specific troubleshooting, if necessary, and for intensive exploration for new placements.

**May 1992 - Hong Kong and Hangzhou**

After flying on May 20th, a Wednesday, from an unusually hot London where the temperature had soared to 90F [I vividly remember Barcelona and Genoa football supporters touring the London streets and Green Park before the onset of their match at Wembley], I reached Hong Kong to find the temperature strangely a mere 84F, six degrees lower than in London. I spent a few days, seeing to the new Hong Kong Project and fulfilling various appointments (see chapter 7). On Tuesday, May 26th, I took the afternoon Dragon flight out of busy Hong Kong to Hangzhou, where Du Jian met me. That evening Xu Yaogen, my host and Du Jian's boss (director of the *jiaowei*'s *waiban*), with his wife gave me dinner at the Xinqiao Hotel where for once I was staying. It was a superb antidote to the humid bustle of Hong Kong. This was followed by a boat trip at dusk on the West Lake (Xi Hu) to an island, where a Song dynasty drama was being performed. I understood little of the action. As far as I could see, a lord was trying to marry his daughter off suitably. The first suitor, an aged man of 98 with a bird in a cage, seemed to be dreaming of a girl enveloped in a cloud of smoke. He was followed by a swordsman, and then by a painter of peonies. All candidates proved unsuitable. Eventually in desperation he chose one of the audience. (I was later told how lucky I

29

was, for they usually choose a visiting foreigner, a *waiguoren*, if possible! I had narrowly escaped.) The show finished at 8.30 and, chilly now, we left, by the boat across the dark lake, lit only by lanterns – a beautiful sight, so soothing after Hong Kong.

The next morning in my hotel I first met briefly the GAPpers from the Institute of Technology, Alison Percy and Emma Lavender, and the first two at Shaoxing, Sarah Richardson and Rachel Bliss – and tried to sort out any problems they had. Then I interviewed the three Zhejiang teachers who were to go to the UK the following September.

**Shanghai**

These meetings over, we set about the main purpose of this particular visit – first, the search for a placement in Shanghai and, second, our follow-up safari to Hunan where we hoped to finalise arrangements. Du Jian had yet again been deputed to accompany me on this mission. We went by train to Shanghai, and, as usual at this stage, I stayed in the still reasonably priced Peace Hotel, while Du Jian stayed at the Music Conservatory. My earlier attempts in Shanghai, visiting No. 3 School in 1990, and in 1991 meeting with Li Shou Pao, the senior YMCA official, had not borne fruit, but on May 29th, Shao Chun Lei, a young official from the Shanghai Association for International Exchanges visited me. At the time I noted him as "a keen young man with the usual Chinese gentility." From him I gathered there was indeed a clear demand for our volunteers, and yet I somehow seemed unable to achieve anything concrete through official channels. That was to come later.

Nevertheless, on this trip, unofficially and quite by chance on 28th May, things did begin to crystallise. Gu Ping, my friend I had first met in Suzhou in 1983, was now lecturing at the prestigious Shanghai Music Conservatory, founded in 1927. He had spoken about us and GAP to Zhang Xianping, head of his *waiban* there, who wanted to provide teachers of English for the Conservatory's music students. Though

30

eventually this proved impossible, the upshot after various meetings was a useful temporary toehold in Shanghai. A pair of GAPpers was to sleep at the Music Conservatory, but teach English, not after all, to the music students, but to the staff of a new hotel, opened in 1991. This was the Jianguo in Cao Xi Lu, opposite the magnificent French-built Catholic cathedral of St. Ignatius in Xu Jia Hui, a burgeoning district of the city, where the Metro was soon to open. Zhang's friend, Chen Hong Jun, was General Manager of the hotel. I inspected the Conservatory's accommodation and the hotel's classroom on the topmost floor above the lifts in the high-rise building. It all looked satisfactory, and we agreed to go ahead. The first and only pair to go there, Polly Davies and Emma Parker, worked there from February to June 1993. In the long run, however, the plan proved unsuccessful, for the hotel staff were not strongly motivated and in any case the management found they could do better with qualified teachers from another source. The arrangement came to an end after one semester. We had, nevertheless, at least expanded into the largest city in China. From then on I used to stay at the Jianguo when in Shanghai (they gave me a favourable rate), and as late as my visit in 2001 some of the staff still remembered the two GAPpers with gratitude. By the time this hotel placement collapsed CAAC, China's airline regulatory body, had come to the rescue. They were so pleased with what GAP was doing in Guangzhou that they invited us, unrequested, to supply volunteers for their Air Polytechnic at Longhua airfield, not far from Xu Jia Hui (see chapter 6).

One afternoon Gu Ping persuaded Du Jian and me to visit the newly opened Nan Pu Bridge over the Huang Pu River, a mighty construction, the first of two vast suspension bridges from Shanghai city to the new Pudong development area. Early one Saturday morning we set off by taxi. The crowds, all Chinese, were waiting in long queues to see this new feat of Chinese engineering. It was a May morning, already hot, and we certainly did not want to stand waiting for hours. Gu Ping promptly went to the officials at the head of the queue, and to my embarrassment told them there was a distinguished foreigner waiting. We were waved to the front. Totally without distinction as I was, and feeling inwardly guilty, in the heat I was nevertheless happy with the arrangement. As we walked across the massive bridge, up the river we could see the shipbuilding yards, and below us the ships, large and small, plying their way up and down. After walking back to the Shanghai side, we took a taxi over to Pudong, then a desolate sight, but destined to be the new financial centre of Shanghai, with the intention of rivalling Hong Kong. Six years later, when I visited Pudong again, all was very different with many high-rise buildings including the Oriental Pearl Television Tower, claimed by some to be the second tallest construction in Asia. Soon the new Shanghai Pudong International Airport would be in operation. We returned through the tunnel back to the Waitan (Bund).

## Changsha (second visit)

In the evening of the same day, Saturday, May 30th, Du Jian and I left for our second visit to Changsha, the provincial capital of Hunan. We had learnt that Hunan as a province was significantly poorer than the coastal provinces, seventeenth out of China's 29. We arrived in the evening to be met again by Li Shihong, Hunan *jiaowei*'s young official who was turning out to be quite a personality. In the car to the hotel he told us how the central government had cracked down on costly hosting of foreign guests, something that had already given me much pause for thought. He also told us there had been confusion over the flights back from Changsha which meant Du Jian and I both had to stay far longer than intended. After initial frustration I was glad, because a day or two longer in Hunan could only be beneficial, and enable us to get the feel of the place as a suitable area for GAP. It was less good for Du Jian, whose Zhejiang colleagues needed him back to cope with an expected Japanese delegation, but there was nothing we could do, and we had to agree to the delay. Du Jian rang Hangzhou and made his peace.

## A Visit to Shaoshan

As the next day was Sunday, neither formal work nor negotiation took place, though unofficially, all day my hosts were probing me about GAP. Instead, Shu Fanqing took us to Shaoshan, Mao's historic birthplace. The road was hair-raisingly rough, but the countryside we passed through was beautiful, undulating, and in the fields there were myriads of workers planting rice. After a long, hot, two-hour drive we reached the fabled valley of Shaoshan, which was now a tourist shrine, a Mecca for the faithful. As today was Sunday, coach loads of Chinese were already there. The peace and tranquillity that the young Mao must have experienced, was totally absent; we could only imagine how it must have been.

First we visited the poetically-named Dripping Water Cave, which was an historic complex of tunnels and dwelling rooms, all guarded by massive steel doors, reminiscent of Lin Biao's hide-out outside Hangzhou. It was here in these subterranean dwellings that Mao and his aides worked for eleven seminal days in June 1966, preparing for the Great Proletarian Cultural Revolution. The Sunday crowds wound in and out of this site, so crucial in their lives; for some it must have been dominant in their memory. It was hot, crowded and unpleasant, but even a foreigner with a sense of history like myself could not but be awestruck by the momentous decisions reached here, decisions that had such an impact, not only on China, but also on the world.

After that we moved on to Mao's birthplace itself, the main shrine of Shaoshan. It was a fairly large peasant house with mud walls, several rooms and a thatched roof. Destroyed by the Guomintang in the Civil War it had apparently been rebuilt in 1956. Certainly there was something artificial, something "spoofy" about it all, but I am sure the ground plan was genuine enough. Certainly the valley was striking and, without the tourist crowds, would have been peaceful – and is still, I was told, on weekdays. Talking to the driver at lunch, I discovered he had spent a year in Lesotho, and had even spent

33

a day in London. Chinese working for government offices are far from insular; they have been about the world.

After lunch we repaired to the museum, rather a dusty place and less appealing, made worse by the press of crowds, the extreme humidity and the tackiness of the Maoist memorabilia on sale. As I pondered on one of the exhibits, I was astonished to hear a voice behind me saying, "You should be proud of Britain. What a wonderful heritage. Your country has done so much for the people and nations of the world." It was Shu, a conservative communist. (The Hunan government I later learned was still classically communist with very little sign of Deng's reforms or of the liberalisation I had seen in the coastal provinces.) So this was an astonishing remark, uncalled for, and apparently genuinely meant. Or was he just sycophantic? I was inwardly, perhaps naively, moved. To have spoken thus to me apparently so genuinely in this "Bethlehem" of Maoism was overwhelming, something to be treasured all my days. We returned to the car. The drive back seemed long in the hot, humid afternoon. We all slept.

The next morning formal negotiations began in earnest. First, we met Madam Gao Shang Zeng, the vice-director of the *jiaowei*, previously a professor of computer studies. She knew a little English, she said, but added ruefully, "My only English is computer programming English, BASIC!" A delightful person, she was yet another example of women reaching very senior official posts despite, I suspect, the continuing cultural subservience of women in many homes. As vice-director of the provincial *jiaowei*, she had major responsibility for the education of all Hunan's population of 64.3 million, roughly the size of the UK. Delightful she may have been, but the negotiations were tough, and the outcome of our talks was not too hopeful. They wanted to send Chinese teachers to the UK from the start, but I could not agree to that – Chinese placements in the UK were in desperately short supply. I explained, with Du Jian's help, that "first best is two-way (exchange); second-best is one way, and third best is no way." Madam Gao was prepared to start on a one-way basis, without sending Chinese to the UK, on one condition, that the *jiaowei* could send a delegation to England at GAP's expense. Naturally I wondered whether this was merely a chance for them to have a free trip to the UK. That is how it seemed to me, and this was something GAP could not countenance. Not only could we not afford it, the principle was wrong. The meeting lasted an eternity, it seemed a long three hours, but ended with an excellent banquet at the Xiangjiang Hotel.

## Yueyang

With a provisional arrangement agreed, accompanied by Li Shihong, we started in the mid-afternoon the long drive to Yueyang, 180 kilometres away on the northern borders of the province and on the eastern banks of the Dong Ting Hu. This lake, at 3,900 sq. km, is reportedly the second largest stretch of fresh water in China. The drive was fascinating, through fabulous countryside, mountains and green paddy fields. As so often in the China of the early 90s, the new arterial road was still under construction, and there were massive worksites with swarms of workers, like ants, building it. At one point there was yet another diversion off through country lanes. We were getting late and a little impatient; we had already endured several of these slow, bumpy diversions, and, as we approached the barrier, Li Shihong leant out of the car window, "We have with us a prestigious foreign official, and we need to get through urgently." Here yet again, as in Shanghai a few days before, I was to act the part of someone important. Despite my embarrassment I did my best, duly inflated myself and sat erect with, I hope, suitable dignity. The traffic controller waved us through, much to my amusement. As the journey continued, and while Du Jian slept, Li Shihong and I had a long chat about Maoism and its principles – always an interesting subject for me. At one point Li announced, "This is the Miluo River" The car stopped, Du Jian immediately awoke, jumped out of the car, full of excitement, and rushed to the side of the bridge. Why this

35

thrill? I could not understand. Then he translated. This is where according to legend the first ever dragon boat race took place hundreds of years ago. In the period of the Warring States (475-221 BC), Qu Yuan, a poet in the Zhou state, and a wise minister much loved by the people, fought against corruption. Dissatisfied, he decided to commit suicide by throwing himself into the Miluo River. Nearby fishermen raced to save him, but in vain. At this time each year, the fifth day of the fifth lunar month (the Double-Fifth), dragon boat races take place in Chinese communities around the world. Special food, *zongzi*, is eaten.

We returned to the car and continued our journey, arriving in Yueyang at 5.15 p.m. Tired and exhausted though we were, we were taken straight into a conference room to brief the president, Professor Li Lingyan, about the GAP programme. He was a delightful man, who turned out to be a competent amateur artist, and had just returned from a fortnight in Vancouver. Zhang Shenglin, one of the lecturers, now interpreting for us, was articulate, humorous, and later a good friend. Nevertheless, the atmosphere without air-conditioning was hot, humid and stifling; we had come straight from a three-hour drive on bumpy roads, I had a headache, and the last thing I wanted to do was to give a briefing, or indeed talk at all. I staggered through an hour of this, after which we went to a restaurant, and had a good supper; we were then taken to our hotel, refreshingly new and comfortable, but, I was carefully assured, extremely costly. Later, despite the heat and humidity, Du Jian and I sauntered down to the lakeside to get some air, but there was little to see and little fresh air to breathe. This was all new to him too. In my room, before retiring to bed, I was able incongruously to watch David Mellor, then Culture Secretary, being interviewed on the BBC TV World Service.

Next morning I woke at 6 a.m. How extraordinary to wake deep in the heart of China, no longer in the coastal provinces, nor even in a provincial capital – a totally new experience for me. After breakfast with Zhang we returned to the college, and were shown the brand new English teaching block and the even newer music and art departments. These were all incredibly more impressive than anything I had seen so far, even in the prosperous east, at, for instance, Shaoxing. The usual statistics came out; there were thirty new practice rooms, thirty pianos and Chinese organs. The college was still being built, and they showed us a model of the completed work. The site was on a beautiful peninsula, bounded by the Dong Ting Lake on three sides with superb views all round. By 10.30 a.m. the sun was extremely strong, and carelessly I was hatless. I noticed the president disappearing back to his office; he returned with his new North American ten-gallon hat for me to wear, much to everyone's amusement. After lunch of turtle – an expensive delicacy – and fresh fish from the lake, Zhang took us to Yueyang Pavilion, the poet Qu Yuan's shrine, and to the nearby dragon boat race stadium. Because the first race ever was paddled near here, this stadium was reportedly the world centre for the sport, and teams come from all over the globe to compete.

At 3 p.m. we started back for Changsha with the Mao-suited, rather austere vice-president, this time not in the *jiaowei*'s smart, comfortable limousine, but in the college's old Shanghai-constructed model. Several times en route we had an engine failure. As we all waited by the roadside on one of these occasions, I noticed the tyres had worn smooth. I surreptitiously pointed this out to Du Jian; who expostulated proudly that Zhejiang, his province, would never allow a foreigner in a car like that! In spite of it all, we arrived safely back at the Xiangjiang Hotel that evening. Yueyang would be an excellent placement, if only the *jiaowei* would agree. For a decision I had to wait for my next visit.

**Nanjing**

Next morning I again felt the incongruity of being in far away Changsha and yet seeing BBC World TV – Denmark by referendum had rejected Maastricht, and, even more historic, Yeltsin had ordered a full imperial funeral in St. Petersburg, for the bodies of Tsar Nicolas II and his wife, just discovered at Ekaterinburg. I flew to Nanjing, where in my brief 24 hours there I met the two volunteers, Annabel Foley and Harriet Baker (Annabel later wrote a good article for the *South China Morning Post*), and the returned Chinese teachers. As Gao Yuemin, this year our co-ordinator for all China, was seriously ill, I spent time discussing GAP arrangements with his temporary replacement, Ding Anning, and then flew home via Hong Kong.

## 4. Journeys to Hubei and Hunan 1992-1993

Late the following October I returned to China for my usual annual inspection. On Wednesday, October 14th, I flew via Copenhagen to Beijing where I fulfilled my usual round there, seeing the Ambassador, Sir Robin Maclaren, visiting the Rolls-Royce office and the Director of the British Council, Adrian Johnston, in his new offices at Landmark.

### Qingdao

That autumn I made visits to Qingdao, where Ben Rogers and Nick Poynder, were in good order, and to Nanjing, where there had been a change. Though both volunteers, Laura Birtwistle and Katie Harmsworth, still lived in Dawn Garden at the Language School, Katie now commuted by cycle to Jingling, a "key" middle school, originally founded by American missionaries in 1888. The atmosphere there was totally different from the Language School for, being unused to foreign teachers, they gave Katie a great welcome and she felt much needed, always an important factor for a GAPper. The 1992 GAP agents' conference was also held in Nanjing, chaired again, as in 1991, by Professor Yuan Xiangwan and me; Gao Yuemin had recovered and was there, though he looked far from well. He resigned soon afterwards and withdrew to business in Hainan − a sad loss for us all.

I then moved on to Hangzhou where there had been another change. The Institute of Technology had not been a success, and the *jiaowei* had now moved the placement to the Zhejiang College of Traditional Chinese Medicine (TCM), and the first GAPpers, Libby Gubba and Becky Husband, had already started. Their task was a supremely challenging one. The president of the college, Madam Ge Yin Li, was running a crash course in English language for the medical professors and lecturers. I watched Libby and Becky teach; they were managing extremely well, for each day they had to teach the same class of senior academics not just simple language, but nuances of meaning between similar words. This was a remarkable improvement on the two previous Hangzhou placements, the Foreign Language School (1990-1991) and the Institute of Technology (1991-1992). Then on October 27th I moved on to Shanghai where I further discussed the placement at the Jianguo Hotel and the Music Conservatory with the General Manager and his Head of Human Resources. Apparently they had great problems with their 1,000 staff; for, as soon as they had learnt enough English, they usually left to join a joint-venture company.

Now that a placement in Hunan province seemed settled, I looked for further expansion – this time in Hubei, the province that lies on the other side of the Dong Ting Lake from Hunan, and to its north. Situated 600 miles upstream from Nanjing, Wuhan is a triple city, made up of Hankou, Wuchang and Hanyang. Heavily industrial previously with foreign concession areas, it was famous for its revolutionary cells in the early twentieth century and for the accidental explosion in October 1911 (known as the "double-tenth") that triggered off the revolution and overthrow of the Qing dynasty. It was here too that Mao Zedong made one of his famous swims in 1956. On October 29th I flew from Shanghai to Wuhan, the provincial capital, not this time with Du Jian, but Sun Haifeng from Qingdao. After a flight of almost two hours we touched down at 9.30 p.m., were met by a Xue Zhong Xiong, a young *jiaowei* official, and taken to the Hong Shan Hotel.

To save expense I had mistakenly refused the offer of the Li Jiang, the only two star hotel in the city, and settled for the Hong Shan, which was appreciably cheaper, and therefore appreciably worse. The choice was poor, the experience rich. The Hong Shan was a typically dreary example of this type of Chinese hotel, and rather dirty too, with carpets heavily tea-stained and punctuated with cigarette-burn holes. I suggested to Sun that we walked to the better two-star hotel, the Li Jiang, next door, to book our breakfast for the morning. As we returned in the dimly-lit streets, the nostalgic sound of British 1940s ballroom dance music assailed our ears. Astonishingly, in the middle of the road was a group of men and women, shod in clumsy, heavy working boots, learning to dance in old ballroom style − quickstep, fox-trot and waltz. The leader, accompanied by a tape, demonstrated a step, and then the whole class joined in. Incongruous though it seemed, these old tunes from my youth, now long ago almost forgotten in the UK, were here alive and well in this grubby, industrial city in Central China. Bourgeois culture equally seemed alive and well.

The next morning after a good Chinese breakfast in the Li Jiang, we arrived at the Hubei *jiaowei's waiban*, rather a tatty building. We talked for three hours with its director, Peng Dao Fu, who, in spite of having just returned from a year's study-leave in London, could not speak a word of English, nor understand any either. We wondered what he had been doing in London, but he was pleasant, courteous, and seemed interested enough. We soon had lunch, at which Sun Hai Feng, as usual, kept up the GAP patter for me in Chinese. He is another first rate ambassador for GAP, like Du Jian, as well as for me yet another friend and support.

I now unexpectedly needed more cash to reimburse Sun Haifeng for his unexpected airfare and expenses (he had intended to come by train). The search for a Bank of China branch which would accept my credit card involved us in a multitude of taxi drives in this vast city. Though now, in 2003, enjoying a boom, in 1992 it was still grey, dirty and heavily industrial. Our taxi journeys took us to all three of its parts. I felt I knew enough of the atmosphere here.

Nor was that the only problem − buying my rail ticket to Yueyang for my evening journey presented further difficulties. The rail station even now was crowded, with vast queues stretching back from the ticket booths. In the end, we discovered there were no soft-seats left on the night trains. All Xue could buy me was a hard-seat ticket for the 10.15 p.m. train, not a good prospect with all my heavy luggage.

Next, Sun Hai Feng and I now took a taxi to look for Iain Pococke, a former 1991 GAPper from Fuzhou, then on a full

Wuhan university course. We took another taxi to the university. With its plenty of trees and small hills the campus was beautiful, a welcome oasis in the dusty dreariness of this shapeless city, but Iain had left only ten minutes before. With these taxi excursions I had had enough of Wuhan to make me realise I had no real wish to return. Sun Hai Feng, whose home was in beautiful Qingdao, totally agreed. GAP would be better elsewhere.

## By rail to Yueyang (from Wuhan)

The time came for me to leave Wuhan. At 9.30 a.m. we departed for the station. It was pitch dark and the waiting area was seething with waiting passengers seated all over the floor, staring as usual at this old foreigner who had just arrived. We passed through into the soft-seat waiting-room which was hardly better. Xue and Sun Hai Feng assured me all would be well; I would get my seat. As the time for the train's arrival approached, the bolts on the massive door onto the platform were thrust back, the door was opened and the crowd surged forward. The train drew in, we could see it was already overcrowded; there was not a hope of getting my reserved hard-seat. Xue and Sun, using their muscle as officious young party cadres, remonstrated with the conductor and tried to get me into No. 1 coach. Not a hope. Even the corridors were overflowing. Eventually the kitchen crew, five jolly cooks, took pity. Beckoning me to climb up into their steaming hot kitchen, a great height from ground level and with no steps, they physically manhandled me up. I clambered on board, and my luggage followed. The cooks took me to the last remaining seat in the restaurant car, a wicker chair. I took it, paid my 15 Yuan (the cost of the seat, tea and later, noodles). I looked round. The car too was crowded and heavy with steam from cooking. I dozed intermittently, overcome by the kindness shown by all the passengers and crew. Remarkably at about 1 a.m. a cook came round offering bowls of hot noodles to have with the tea I had already been sipping since

42

arrival. There would have been no such service on British Rail, I thought.

Then after four hours in the hot, steamy atmosphere, as we approached Yueyang, I had to concoct a plan for extricating myself. One fellow-passenger, dressed typically in a Mao cap, kindly advised me to make my way along the passage to the exit. There was no hope of that. The corridors were stacked full of people. The attendant said "Qing zuo," as someone gave up his seat for me. Everybody showed such consideration. Then it was the turn of the five cooks to take pity on this poor elderly foreigner; they beckoned me through their kitchen still threateningly hot from their inferno-like coke oven. They helped me with the luggage to the open space by the exit. (Kitchens on Chinese trains have no doors, for they need maximum ventilation in the heat of cooking; instead they merely have a bar across the exit to prevent accidental falls onto the line.)

As the train stopped I jumped to the ground onto the dark, ill-lit platform – it seemed a terrible drop. They then cast down all my baggage, but, disaster, my brief case fell into the pitch darkness under the train. It was 3 a.m. There was much shouting. People rallied round, and one passenger dived under the train and retrieved my case. What a mercy, for it had all my documentation and notes for my placements. At the station exit Zhang Shenglin from the teachers' college met me. A blessed relief – the journey had been an experience. With small luggage or a backpack, it would have been less of a problem and acceptable, but with my heavy baggage it was quite an ordeal, much ameliorated by the constant kindness of my Chinese fellow-passengers and the cooks. That is my abiding memory. It was now 3.15 a.m., still dark. Zhang and I went straight to the hotel, and I was let into my room.

## Yueyang (second visit)

Thus my second visit to Yueyang began. Next day, October 31st, I talked again with President Li Lingyan in the morning to make final arrangements for the arrival of the first GAPpers

43

the following February. I also talked for an hour with a group of eight third year students, something I always enjoy doing. In the afternoon we visited Jun Shan Island, which at this time of year, the autumn, is no longer surrounded by water from Dong Ting Lake. (The frosts and snow on the higher levels of the Himalayas in the autumn and winter months prevent a water flow. When the snows melt in spring and summer, the lake fills.) We returned to Zhang's flat in No. 1 Middle School where his wife was teaching. I was introduced to their three year-old son, Dong Dong, who welcomed me in brilliant, perfectly-accented English, "Good afternoon, how are you?" I replied suitably to this astonishing little boy. Later in the evening I went out to a meal with them; as often happens, they insisted on paying, with the usual comment, "but this is our country."

The next morning I left by train for Changsha. At my two-hour meeting there in the *jiaowei waiban* with Shu Fanqing and Li Shihong they agreed to a GAP placement, but with a proviso – they, the *jiaowei*, should be invited as a delegation to the UK. The negotiation was again tough, and I undertook to try for this, but I could promise nothing until I had reported back to the GAP office in UK. The upshot was a trial run for an initial two years, while I did my best to fulfil their wishes. (In the end, much as I tried on their behalf, I failed, and we sadly lost Yueyang, the best of all placements so far, after a mere three semesters.) After a superb banquet, hosted by Madam Gao, the Director, I had hoped for a quiet evening, but it was not to be. Li Shihong (a delightful, but rather intense, young man), who had recently been to the US and Thailand, insisted on coming to my room to discuss yet again the respective merits and demerits of capitalism and socialism.

The next morning I flew directly to Fuzhou for a few days, where Bob Allen, the sole GAPper at No. 1 School, was relishing being on his own (his colleague had left a few days after arrival in October, and Bob had refused my offer of a replacement, so that he could gain most out of his situation).

44

He had integrated remarkably well and was teaching splendidly. I remember he took me to a vast cave, carved out of the mountain as a nuclear shelter, but now used as a dance hall – a fascinating occasion. He also had had the initiative to ask for some teaching in a well-equipped kindergarten near his school, and to have lessons in bamboo painting, one of which I watched. The following Christmas Day he was the subject of a two-page article in *The Guardian* by Simon Winchester. After his placement he spent another seven or eight months travelling in China, possibly longer than any other volunteer, before reading Chinese at Cambridge. After Cambridge he spent many years pursuing his Chinese interests, both in China and Taiwan. From Fuzhou I flew home via Shenzhen and Hong Kong where I attended the official opening, by the Prince of Wales, of CELL in Kennedy Town, where a Hong Kong GAPper, Richard Wright, was teaching (see chapter 7).

My night in Shenzhen was an eye-opener. This city had only been founded a few years before by Deng Xiao Ping as part of his liberalising economic policy. Just across the land border from Hong Kong, it had its own special protected zone; Chinese could not enter with out a special pass. I disliked the place. It had all the busyness and capitalist ethos of Hong Kong but without any of its brilliance and glitter. Without denying the evident achievement of its rapid construction, Shenzhen was for me a pale, tawdry shadow of its great neighbour.

**April 1993 Shanghai and Yueyang (third visit)**

In April 1993 I flew out to Shanghai and Yueyang again. Our two GAPpers at Shanghai, Polly Davis and Emma Parker, who lived at the Music Conservatory, were much in demand by these high grade Chinese students of western classical music who needed English for their international commitments. Unfortunately that part of the placement could not continue as funding from central government for language training was not forthcoming. In any case, at the Jianguo

Hotel where most of their teaching was supposed to take place in a classroom high above the lift floors, many of the staff who attended seemed to lack motivation, and our GAPpers became bored. The future looked rather bleak. That April I stayed for the first time in the Jianguo, and it was to become my base in Shanghai until the end of the decade. In April 2001 some Jianguo staff still remembered these GAPpers and their usefulness.

While there, I received a visit from Richard Thorne who, on behalf of Rolls-Royce, ran the English language training for the CAAC. He told me that our Guangzhou placement had worked so well that CAAC now wanted me to make an arrangement with CAAC's Air Polytechnic for training ground staff, which was at the old Longhua Airfield only a short distance away from the Jianguo. Richard and I immediately visited the school in torrential rain. I had a meal with the delightful principal, Zhang Zexian, at a restaurant near the Longhua Pagoda. When I told him that I realised that he would have to get approval from CAAC's headquarters in Beijing, he replied, "No. They have approved already, as they approved of GAP's work in Guangzhou." The first GAPpers were to arrive the following September 1993. This was to become one of our most long-lasting placements and remained so until my departure in 1999. At last we had a firm foothold in Shanghai, and this was to remain.

Our first volunteers to Yueyang, Patrick Foulis and Jonathan Millard, had gone out in February 1993, and in April I visited them there. The placement was proving a great success in all ways; the teaching was effective, the accommodation excellent and the relationship with staff and pupils could not be bettered. The standard of English among the students was the highest I had yet encountered; Patrick Foulis was able to give a lecture-style class at almost normal speed on English marriage, giving examples from, for instance, Jane Austen. On the Sunday we crossed the lake by a 40-minute ferryboat ride to Jun Shan Island in the Dong Ting Lake. The next day, April 19th, I flew back from

Changsha to Hong Kong, where I spent a few days handing over the Hong Kong project to Richard Edwards (see chapter 7). I arrived home on April 26th.

## October/November 1993

By the summer it was clear that the Yueyang placement in Hunan was a success, even if its lifespan was at the mercy of the bargaining postures of the *jiaowei*. I was now keen to find another inland province for GAP. My visit to Hubei in October 1992 had already proved to me that there was little hope for GAP there, so I decided to look even further west, and my thoughts turned to Sichuan, a vast province then, before Chongqing was made autonomous, with a population of some 112,000,000; I was told that if it was an independent country, it would be the eighth largest in the world. Roughly the size of France in landmass, it has in the east one of the densest rural populations in the world and to the west the sparsely populated mountain areas bordering on Tibet. With its irrigation system it has for millennia been one of the wealthiest parts of China. In 1984 it was here that Zhao Ziyang experimented with the "responsibility system" in agriculture. Furthermore, Deng Xiao Ping was a Sichuanese from Guanghan. Though my planned annual visit in autumn 1993 already seemed likely to be the most extensive I had ever undertaken, I nevertheless added an exploratory visit to Sichuan at the end.

I flew out from Heathrow on October 11th to Shanghai (via Hong Kong), and for the second time stayed at the Jianguo Hotel where our GAPpers had previously worked. I had now abandoned the Peace Hotel where the prices were rising steeply. (Jianguo gave me a favourable discount, and became my base in Shanghai for the next six or seven years.) On my first morning Shao Chun Lei, from the City's International Exchange Office (who had previously visited me in the Peace Hotel), took the trouble to cycle out to have a chat. It was good to have his support, and to know that there was still interest from the Shanghai authorities. Nothing, however, as yet came of it. Meanwhile, despite the failure of the Jianguo-Music Conservatory experiment the future for something in Shanghai was already assured by the start of the Longhua placement. It had started superbly. During my stay I watched our first two GAPpers, Tom Fairley and Edward Duffus, teaching competently, and the college seemed pleased. CAAC's contentment with GAP's work was soon to lead to further development in Sichuan and at Tianjin.

But another Shanghai facet of our arrangements had only a little time to run. Since the beginning we had made it mandatory for GAPpers, after six weeks in China, to travel to Shanghai for registration at the consulate-general. This worked effectively and beneficially for all in the first years, especially when the numbers were few, only six each half-year at first, and the distances relatively small – from Nanjing, Hangzhou and Fuzhou. It was, moreover, much enjoyed by the volunteers, and gave them experience of Chinese travel after only a few weeks. By this time, 1993, however, the scene was entirely different. The numbers were rising substantially – there were already sixteen each half-year – it was becoming increasingly difficult to administer these numbers in Shanghai, despite all the help we had from the Consulate and the British Council. For that reason alone I realised the rendezvous would have to stop, but this was not the only problem. The distances were now greater – from as far away as Guangzhou, Qingdao and now even Yueyang in Central China, which entailed a long boat journey of several days down the Yangtze much as they enjoyed that. I could also see that soon, perhaps, GAPpers would have to come from Chengdu and other parts of Sichuan, and that would be expensive and virtually impossible in the timeframe allowed. On this occasion, October 1993, I met them all as they came in at the East China Normal University where they were staying. It was a treat for me to be there. They had last seen each other in Beijing, and here they were after six weeks' work and, for some of them, long journeys, greeting each other, excitedly swapping stories of those first weeks in a rich diversity of places – Fuzhou, Guangzhou, Nanjing, Hangzhou, Shaoxing, Qingdao and now far away Yueyang. Most arrived by train, but those from Guangzhou, Fuzhou and Qingdao came by ship. For me this was fascinating, but it was destined to be the last official GAP reunion in Shanghai.

From Shanghai I travelled to Hangzhou for two exploratory journeys in Zhejiang; the aim here was to spread out from the capital city. I had already negotiated at Shaoxing Teacher's College in October 1991 for GAPpers to work there in alternate semesters, and the first ones, Jane Alexander and Andrea Ledward, had gone there the following February (1992). Though I had seen them in Hangzhou, I had seen neither them nor their successors, Sarah Richardson and Rachel Bliss, on site. By September the Zhejiang *jiaowei* had agreed to increase the frequency, so that we sent GAPpers to Shaoxing each term. Consequently this autumn, 1993, I was able to reach the city and see Sally Nash and Anne-Marie Critien, the current pair, in action. It confirmed my opinion that this was an excellent placement.

But the aim now was to expand within Zhejiang, or rather to replace the TCM, which was soon to complete its "crash" English training course, with another teachers' college outside Hangzhou. The *jiaowei* consequently took me to the college at Huzhou, another ancient city which reportedly shares with Hangzhou the reputation of being the original home of silk. It had recently become part of a special economic development zone. Here on Sunday, October 17th, the welcome was as warm and familiar as usual; a band of students stood clapping my arrival with notices saying "Welcome Mr Marshall" etc. I had a successful negotiation with the principal, Professor Cai Qing Jiang. The college was smaller than Shaoxing, but the atmosphere was quite as good, and was to be another outstanding placement, beginning in February 1994. After the negotiations, I was shown (sadly in the pouring rain) the unique double pagoda of 800 AD, a stone pagoda encased within a wooden one. Though the distance was only 88 kilometres, the drive back to Hangzhou took a long three hours on crowded wet roads with many road works. From February 1994 Zhejiang's GAPpers would all be outside the provincial capital. This was an excellent development, not yet followed by Jiangsu and Fujian.

My eight-hour train journey next day to Nanjing was in a soft-sleeper where I found myself having discussions with a Zhejiang TV crew, and then after Shanghai, watching a young mother and her five year old child, playing a Chinese version of Monopoly (*Xinbanqiang Shouqi*). Capitalism here is even played on board games, and this so soon after Mao's death. I arrived at Nanjing at 6 p.m.

## Nanjing

The next day in Nanjing, after seeing our GAPpers, Helen Shariatmadari and Tania Weldon, in the Foreign Language School and Jinling respectively, I visited the headquarters of the Amity Foundation, a charity funded by religious organisations around the world, which supplies teachers and social workers for needy places in China. Its chairman was the son of Bishop Ding Guan Sun (K.H.Ting), Chairman of the Three Self Movement, the non-Catholic group of churches. At the *jiaowei* there was talk of GAP's expansion within Jiangsu to the prospering areas of Suzhou and Wuxi – this time there would be no need of reciprocation. That was good news indeed.

I travelled to Beijing where I picked up Susan who had just arrived from London, called at the Embassy to report progress and, at GAP HQ's request, to discuss briefly the feasibility of having a placement in Tibet. They advised us to speak to the US Consul-General in Chengdu when we got there, which we eventually did. We then moved on to Qingdao where the 1993 GAP conference was held. At No. 9 School Rhodri Evans and Chris Foye were working well. Rhodri had a beautiful Welsh lilt which the class followed with an equally entrancing lilt "My mother is a secretary".

## Yueyang (fourth visit)

From Qingdao we flew straight to Changsha for my fourth visit to Yueyang. After a long five-hour − it should have been three − car journey from Changsha Airport on poor and crowded roads we arrived at Yueyang Teachers' College about 7 p.m. What I remembered previously as a scenic drive was marred by the pelting rain and heavy traffic. When we arrived, conditions were bleak, the rain was pouring down, the buildings dark and, even worse, the door of our flat was locked and nobody could find the key. As we stood waiting, many people scurried round, trying to help. We were tired, cold and wet. At last, I impatiently put the cases back in the car and, forgetting my normal rule of courtesy in China, rather rudely demanded to be taken to a hotel. Pi (Peter) immediately exclaimed, "Oh. Don't do that. My director will be very annoyed." Just then the standers-by managed to open the door. The room was all ready for us, complete with a bowl of oranges, slippers by the beds, toothpaste and toothbrush. With good grace we accepted.

The next morning we had breakfast in the staff dining room. Bitterly cold though it was, all the doors and windows were open to rid the place of damp. After seeing Richard Holmes and Noel Casey, both fully competent people, teach, we had another tour of the college with the president, Professor Li Lingyan, especially to see the new art facilities. Even more memorable was his tour of the college orangery where we gorged ourselves on oranges straight from the trees, and to his apartment where we saw his latest paintings; he is no mean artist himself. The following morning, Saturday, October 30th, I had my third visit to Jun Shan Island, but this time, the water was minimal, compared with last April; snow and heavy frosts on the higher reaches were now preventing the flow of water into the lake. We enjoyed the walk in the bamboo woods and seeing the monkeys leaping from branch to branch, and the centuries old (perhaps even 800 year-old) tortoise.

51

That evening we once again had to brave the railway, this time from Yueyang to Changsha. Formidable traffic jams on the way to the station and the incredible crowds at Yueyang station made even this a tough experience. The fact that the stationmaster was Professor Li's brother-in-law gave us some encouragement, and we were soon in the soft-seat waiting room. Our train was billed as four hours late. We had the prospect of a long wait ahead of us, and went out into the station forecourt for a bowl of rice. Soon, however, better news came that the Beijing-Guangzhou express was about to arrive. We decided to take it. The doors on to the platform were opened and, as before at Wuhan in April, the deluge of people poured forth onto the platform, but this time we were guided satisfactorily. We paid for two soft-sleeper places for the short journey to Changsha. It was well worth it. Our only companion was a Taiwanese businessman, working in Beijing. So nervous was he of Air China flights to Guangzhou that he always took the long train journey for his circuitous route from Beijing to Taiwan via Hong Kong. We spent the night in Changsha, and flew to Fuzhou the next morning.

**Fuzhou**

With Hunan working satisfactorily my aim now was to see what Sichuan, and its capital, Chengdu, had to offer. At Fuzhou I paid my usual visits to the two middle schools and watched our GAPpers teach; Alastair Smith on idioms and Angus Melville on vampires and other mysteries connected with Halloween. For the Sichuan journey, Qiu Bing, Fujian's GAP agent, had been deputed to accompany us, much as Gao Yuemin had done in Tianjin, Du Jian in Changsha and Sun Haifeng in Wuhan. We were to fly from Xiamen in the south of Fujian. First we spent a whole day driving down through the spectacular Fujian countryside to the city, lunching en route at Quangzhou Overseas Chinese University, and on the way passing vast brickfields, belching forth massive palls of black smoke – a heavily polluted area. Nevertheless the beauty of Xiamen's Portuguese and Dutch architecture much impressed me. The next morning, November 5th, we went to the beach and also visited the delightful Gulangyu Island with its little streets. Here we could just see some outlying islands of Taiwan, Jinmen and Xiao Jinmen, so close to Xiamen. Little wonder there was so much tension here in the 1950s; now apparently Xiamen itself benefits massively from Taiwan's economy. This was a pleasant interlude before Sichuan.

## Chengdu (November 1993)

Susan, Qiu Bing and I flew to Chengdu that evening to be met by Tan Jun, one of the Sichuan *jiaowei* officials whose second language was German. I was later to get to know him better as a good friend, but, as we drove into the centre of Chengdu, Tan Jun and Qiu Bing were busy making arrangements for the next day. Little did we realise how much they would be to the detriment of my main exploratory aim.

Very early next morning, Saturday, Susan and I met Donald Camp, the American consul-general, at his consulate to discuss the possibilities of having GAP in Tibet, as our Beijing embassy had recommended. But the general upshot, as I expected and in fact rather hoped, was that with so much else to go for in China it would be unwise to contemplate all the extra problems posed by Tibet, altitude sickness and a sensitive political situation. (At the time of writing (2003), there are still no GAP placements in Tibet, despite pressure from colleagues, and my own private visit there in 1998.) We met Qiu Bing outside. Though I wanted to get into negotiations straightaway with the *jiaowei*, we began a full day of unintended sightseeing, including the magnificent Wenshu Temple, and the poet Du Fu's cottage.

We were told the *jiaowei* could not see us until 4 p.m., but when we did arrive at that time, we were late, so late that the director of the *jiaowei*, Madam Professor Fu, impatient at having been kept waiting, had left for home. Furthermore, Cai Li, the vice-director of the *waiban*, a fluent English speaker, told us that if we had come in the morning we could have fulfilled our wish and seen a middle school; Qiu Bing's hijacking of the whole day was at the time little short of infuriating. As there was frustratingly no more to discuss at this stage, and it was now the weekend, we were unable to do more. On my next visit to China I would have to fly especially to Chengdu and start afresh. I had come a long way, and nothing had been achieved. Cai Li became, and remains, a good friend. On November 7th Susan and I flew to Guangzhou, saw Charles Coghlan and James Floyer, and returned home.

## 5. Establishment in Sichuan 1994-1995

The following May (1994) I was in China again, visiting both the first GAPpers at Huzhou, Alice Grattan and Isobel Byrne-Hill, and those at Shanghai CAAC Polytechnic, Ben Tait and Peter Clasen. There seemed to be no problems. In addition, I negotiated for new places at schools in the two Jiangsu cities; Wuxi (No.12 Professional), and Suzhou (Garden School).

The main purpose of the visit, however, was to return to Sichuan to complete negotiations, so abbreviated the previous November. On Wednesday, May 25th, I flew from Shanghai to Chengdu in a comfortable Boeing 757 to restart my dialogue with the Sichuan *jiaowei*. In the aircraft loos I remember reading the charmingly written notice, "Timely Rinse Toilets after using"! After the three-hour flight of 1700 kilometres to Chengdu, Tan Jun, my last year's interpreter, met me. I again spent the night at the Sichuan Hotel. There was now much noisy construction work in progress next-door; I later discovered this was to be the new 28-storey Holiday Inn. I remember waking at 4 a.m. and, sleepless, whiling away the time yet again, with BBC World Service – on this occasion Michael Buerke presenting an episode of his *999* series in which a child drowned in a swimming pool.

### Chengdu FLS

The Sichuan *jiaowei* now fulfilled what they had planned for me the previous November. First, Tan Jun took me to a middle school in the suburbs, newly redesignated as a Foreign Language School. It was now awaiting construction and development. The vice-principal, Ran Shao Kang, formerly of Chongqing Foreign Language School, proudly showed me the model of the proposed new building. I could see that one day, this would be an ideal placement, but as yet the accommodation was unsuitable, and I needed to see how things developed before committing myself. As I was leaving, I noticed a hut where many people were hard at work making clothes. I asked the vice-principal if the school got bright students to do manual work, as part of their all-round education. "Oh no," he replied. "Those aren't students, but workers employed by the school. This is our own factory for making suits and other clothes to sell in Germany. Through this we can pay for improvements to our school." Though I suppose I should not have been, I was astonished. I had often heard of entrepreneurial work done by government bodies, such as the PLA (the army), but here was my own first tangible evidence of it. Where public money falls short, private enterprise enters to increase school income for projected developments. Capitalism rules after all, even in the state sector.

**Carehome School**

The second school we visited that day was, by contrast, totally entrepreneurial. In the afternoon Tan Jun took me to Carehome on the Airport Road, a private school where parents paid substantial fees. The visit was fascinating, though in the long run fruitless from GAP's point of view. On arrival we were immediately shown into the newly-built staff-common room, reminiscent, it then seemed to me, of a nightclub, complete with mock Corinthian columns.

Zhang Jian, a young middle school teacher, lively, knowledgeable and fluent in English, who doubled as the owner's secretary, was my first contact. He introduced me to the headmaster, Gan Zheng Huan, a quiet, worn-looking man, probably in his late 50s, and a contrasting figure, the school's owner, Zou Jia, dubbed the Chairman. He was youngish and lively, about 38, very much the typical entrepreneur. Like the headmaster, he seemed to have no English. Before we had spoken for long, in came a third apparently significant member of the group. He was Professor Zhang Yong Ping, who was, it turned out, a governor of the school.

Zhang was a delightful man, quietly spoken, aged about 65, who had held the Chair of Hydrology at Sichuan University of Science and Technology in Chengdu. Born in Hong Kong where his father was a telegrapher, he returned to

China as a small boy with his family in 1936 before World War II. Though Russian was his first foreign language – he had written academic papers in it – he had taught himself English which he spoke fluently and faultlessly, had spent two years in the US and had done four months' research at Dundee.

His particular expertise was on the water flow of the River Yangtze, and it was he who inspired me later to visit the ancient irrigation scheme, Dujiang Yan, outside Chengdu. It had been built in the third century BC by the engineer, Li Bing. Still working after 2,200 years and still being developed, it both controlled the flow of the mighty Min River at flood times and diverted the overflow through channels to irrigate the plains of Sichuan, which had thus become one of the main rice bowls of China. Originally covering one million hectares the system had trebled in size since the communist takeover in 1949. The professor and I had a long talk about all this and about his worries over the Three Gorges Dam, which he feared would affect not only its immediate neighbourhood, but perhaps even Shanghai. He spoke of the city's floods in recent years due to sinking land, the reduction of sedimentation and change in flow. This would only get worse. As an academic hydrologist, he related the problem to the punishing after-effects of the Aswan High Dam in Egypt. This was a stimulating and revealing conversation. (Later, in May 1995, I was taken to see this ancient irrigation scheme; it was a remarkable sight.)

Zou Jia, the chairman, now took me in his shiny Cadillac Sedan to see the school itself. It was astonishing. All the existing buildings had been constructed in the previous four months – classrooms, a medical centre, a large swimming pool and a theatre. There were already 370 pupils at the school, with 700 expected the following year and eventually about 1100, aged between 7 and 18. The children, all boarders, came from every part of China, though mostly from the Chengdu area. Back in the study I felt revolted by the display of wealth and the thought of all these Chinese *nouveau riche* children herded together and closeted away from the rest of society in what was nominally a socialist state. Nevertheless, at the end of my four-hour visit the evident sense of enthusiasm and dedication, shown by the management, deeply impressed me.

At 5.30 p.m., to the accompaniment of Beethoven's Fifth, Zou Jia drove us in his Cadillac to a restaurant in central Chengdu, strangely called "Shenshang-Mister". Kunming dishes were ordered, for Gan is Yunnanese. Round the table the fascinating chat continued with Zou Jia, Gan, Professor Zhang, Tan Jun and the driver; the professor was now the interpreter. Over this exquisite meal the conversation ranged in part over the Cultural Revolution. The professor, as an academic, had been sent to the fields for two or three years. Zou Jia, only eleven in 1966, enrolled as a junior Red Guard, and lost all his education. Now I saw the connection. One of the Red Guards' chief targets in 1966 had been Gan, his Russian teacher, and now, in 1994, Carehome's headmaster. Zou Jia watched the older Red Guards lambasting, taunting, abusing and placarding Gan, because his father had been a Guomintang general. From the professor I heard how much Gan suffered; his life was a misery. After losing all his education from the age of 11, Zou Jia, once things settled down, became a skilled professional photographer. That was his breakthrough. Starting a small photographic shop, he then took part in land speculation and construction. He clearly impressed the professor for not reinvesting all his money in more land and speculation, but instead deciding to devote it to education, to giving Chinese children what he had missed. I was rather more sceptical; I suspected there was plenty of money to be made in education too. Towards the end of the meal Zou Jia suddenly and surprisingly addressed me in English. "I have given you this meal, because I was so impressed by what you told me about GAP's ideals. We hope you send more than two volunteers here." I told him I was much impressed by him and his colleagues. While they had suffered so much, I by comparison had had a soft life, though

58

I still remembered Hitler's bombing of Bristol in particular, and the nightly drone of German planes making for the Midlands. Zou Jia drove me back to the Sichuan hotel. I was mightily impressed, or rather, fascinated, by the interesting counterpoint between these three men – first the youngish, ambitious entrepreneur, secondly his old teacher, now his worn middle-aged headmaster, and thirdly the distinguished academic with an international reputation. So started my brief association with Carehome, which, despite its untimely end, had a fascinating beginning. The next morning at the *jiaowei,* Cai Li and I agreed to go ahead with Carehome provisionally for one semester; I would then review the situation. GAP now in any case had a toehold in Sichuan which was excellent.

## Guanghan Flying College

But through Rolls-Royce's support there was another possibility in Sichuan. CAAC had let me know through Rolls-Royce that they wanted me to visit the Civil Aviation Flying College (CAFC) at Guanghan, an hour away from Chengdu. The next day Tan Jun and I met the college authorities, led by Zhang Zelong, the Dean of Studies, and others. Having heard of our work in Guangzhou and Shanghai, they were already keen for us to start as soon as September or February. This would be the third CAAC placement in China, making a total of two placements overall in Sichuan. After a lunch banquet complete with strawberries, their first of the season, we returned to Chengdu.

## The Sichuan Vice-Director

Now came a key moment. Before setting the seal on our agreement with Sichuan I had to meet the vice-director of the *jiaowei,* Professor Fu Zhongyin, whom I had disgracefully kept waiting the previous autumn and had therefore not met. She invited me with Cai Li and Tan Jun to an evening dinner at a new hotel on the outskirts of Chengdu. A delightful, vivacious, but physically diminutive woman, she turned out to be a renowned western medical academic, a cardiologist, specialising in coronary heart disease, about which she had written many academic papers. Apart from her heavy administrative load as the *jiaowei*'s vice-director – if independent, Sichuan would then have been the eighth most populous country in the world - and her role as a mother of two daughters, she still had her posse of Master's Degree research students each week.

The dinner in the beautiful new restaurant was a welcome relaxation after a hard day; the wine and food were of first class quality. But then suddenly I became aware of the serious working nature of the meal. In the midst of our conversational pleasantries she suddenly and unexpectedly subjected me to rapier-like interrogation about GAP itself; about its funding, the ability of the volunteers, their academic standards and so on. So totally unexpected was this, so searching the questions, that I was momentarily taken aback. But then, as quickly as it had started, the moment was over, and all was well. The meal ended in the splendidly relaxed way in which it had begun, and I returned to my hotel. The Sichuan placement was approved. Back in my room it was a strange contrast to watch on my TV Michael Palin's train journey from Bombay to Madras, part of his round the world in eighty days. The next morning I left for Hong Kong and home. The May 1994 expedition had yielded considerable results, the possibility of a new placement in Zhejiang and certainly two, perhaps more, in Sichuan. A fruitful visit. Westward expansion was really under way, without the doubts cast by Hunan.

**October/November 1994**

The following autumn my regular inspection yielded yet another new placement. By this time the project had been working for over four years, it was growing faster than I expected, and I began to feel that for GAP's sake I should resign from the "lead" role within the next year – five years is the normal maximum length of a GAP project manager's term and I was approaching the age of 65. Yet I enjoyed the work so much that ideally I would like to have kept a little of the project going myself, and hand over the rest. This is in fact what happened.

I arrived in Beijing on October 19th, visited the embassy and Rolls Royce as usual. At Qingdao and Nanjing the volunteers, Tim Pearman, Phylip Scott, Sarah Pollet and Rachel Taylor were all a great success. At Qingdao No. 9 School the headmaster made a special point of telling me how much the school owed to GAP for its substantial progress in English language, and this was recognised in national examinations. They had by then had fourteen of our GAPpers, and in return he had already sent six of his teachers of English to the UK, each for a year, under our scheme. These two components had produced this remarkable improvement.

In Nanjing I also met for the first time Stephen He Xingchu; a new *jiaowei* officer, aged 22 and straight from university; a bright young man with a tremendous sense of humour and impressive enthusiasm for GAP. He was to become one of the mainsprings of GAP, Jiangsu's equivalent of Du Jian of Zhejiang. From there I visited the two new placements in Suzhou, No. 7 Professional High School and Jingfan Middle School where the two Nicky's (Daft and Shaw) were teaching. Jiangsu's first expansion beyond Nanjing was working well. After seeing the two at the Shanghai CAAC, Chris Stewart and James Hamilton, I travelled by rail to Hangzhou, where I was to visit another new placement, part of Zhejiang's internal expansion – the Teachers' College at Li Shui in the south of Zhejiang.

Whereas Shaoxing and Huzhou, GAP's two current placements in Zhejiang, were within easy striking distance of the provincial capital, Hangzhou, the new one to replace Shaoxing, Li Shui, was far in the south of the province. About 450 kilometres away, it was then, before improved road and train communications, so remote from Hangzhou, so comparatively backward and mountainous that it was locally known as "Zhejiang's Tibet". A visit there at that time meant a long, arduous drive on bad roads, for there was still no motorway or rail, though both were being built.

61

When I arrived at Hangzhou, Dan Large, one of the two Li Shui GAPpers who had arrived late – his mother had been seriously injured, almost fatally, in a car accident – was awaiting my arrival there to join his pair, Will Kendall, at Li Shui. He, Du Jian and I travelled there from Hangzhou together. The road passed through beautiful countryside, at first through green rice fields, then through rice harvesting with the mown crops drying in the sun beside the road. After nine hours, at 8 p.m., we arrived at Li Shui, a beautiful little town – Li Shui means "beautiful water" – with old pedal trishaws and hardly a motor vehicle. I was immediately shown to the GAPpers' rooms, which were almost opulent – in reality they had been prepared for eventual future Amity teachers – and met Will Kendall, the other GAPper, who so far had been on his own. It was a great reunion. This was my first visit to Li Shui. I had waived my normal rule, and allowed the placement to start without my seeing it; my trust in the Zhejiang *jiaowei* was justified. I explained GAP's philosophy to the principal, Shi Yang Min, a jolly man with a roundish face; I then had talks with the students and a prolonged discussion at night with the two GAPpers.

The return journey on Monday, November 31st, was again long, but interesting. Not only was the terrain beautiful in the autumn sun, but we had a fascinating interlude at a small town called Najiang (not its real name). Here I met contacts who gave us early lunch in a restaurant. The latter (we will call him Zhang, not his proper name), a short, stocky man, had formerly been a practitioner of traditional Chinese medicine, but he had now turned entrepreneur, a typical example of the new boom-time wealthy middle class. I was on Zhang's right and the town mayor on his left. Over a pre-prandial drink of bird's nest cordial, which I found nauseating, he told me his circumstances. The mayor on his left was his close friend, controlling the town's planning applications, and thus ensuring that Zhang had the monopoly of development. He had built a hundred houses in the last two years, and was in the process of building for himself and his one-child family a large, prestigious detached four-storey house which he took me to see. The following year he hoped to make one million yuan, and after that annually even more.

Then in came another guest resplendent in military-style uniform with colourful badges of rank, who turned out to be the Chief of Police. To my great surprise he greeted me with the old-fashioned courtesy of clasped hands first one side and then the other, the first time in all my travels I had experienced it. He plied me with yet another dose of the sickening bird's nest beverage. So here, as I saw it, was the triumvirate who hand-in-glove could control the little town's building development, and at the same time make plenty of money for themselves. Here was "Chinese socialism" again! Du Jian later told me of his disapproval. After this interlude we drove on, and arrived at Hangzhou at about 6 p.m.

After a couple of nights in Fuzhou visiting the two middle schools and the two GAPpers, John Hay and Alex Thornton, who were in excellent form, I flew on Friday evening, November 4th, to Chengdu, where I was to consolidate our placement position. Though met by Tan Jun again, I was this time to be in the hands of the rather older, kindly, but wearisome Liu Hang. When I met Cai Li at the *jiaowei* the next morning I repeated my reservations over Carehome and my preference for teachers' colleges, as spearheaded by Zhejiang. Apparently, however, the American Peace Corps staffed most of these college English language posts in Sichuan, but in one, at Neijiang, for the moment there was none, and he immediately made plans for my first visit there. Back at the hotel it was, by contrast, refreshing to have BBC World Service and watch Ken Baker's programme on eighteenth century political cartoonists, on Pitt, Fox, North. In Europe it seemed the Bosnian Serbs were threatening all out war.

The Li Shui excursion the week before may have seemed arduous, but that was an easy amble compared with my journey to Neijiang, my second long, wearying return car drive in a fortnight. Neijiang was well to the south of

Chengdu on the way to Chongqing. Liu Hang and I began the tedious and uncomfortable drive at 8.15 a.m. The road was tough, winding and punctuated with seemingly endless, sickening traffic jams. The pall of fog, so typical of central Sichuan, hung over us. In the fields there was no longer rice as in Zhejiang, but millet, cotton and tobacco. To make matters worse, Liu Hang, kind though he was, was no easy travelling companion. He had had a tragic past and, like a taut spring, he could never relax, and never ceased talking about himself the whole way. With a brief stop for a simple Sichuan-style lunch in a small roadside café we arrived at the college on the outskirts of Neijiang after seven hours. Though it had been a draining journey, just as at Yueyang, I was immediately catapulted into negotiations with the president, He Si Xuan, a quiet, kindly man. With him was his deputy, Liu Mei Ju, short, thin and energetic who was soon to succeed as president. Madam Luo, the Head of English, made up the agreeable trio. As they had never had foreign teachers at all, they were keen from the outset and gave us a big welcome. Cai Li's advice back in Chengdu had been correct. (The American Peace Corps volunteers arrived at Neijiang in September 1995. Concentrating on the more specialised work, they were older, more experienced university graduates who were to spend two years in their placements, and were most helpful to our GAPpers. I had a useful meeting with their Project Manager, Don McKay, over supper with the head of English, Madam Luo.)

Conditions at the college were primitive, rather grey; some would say dreary and depressing. Neijiang city itself nearby was likewise grey and forbidding, but the students, mostly from rural, peasant families, were delightful, courteous and eager. For the more resilient, enterprising GAPper I could see this would be an excellent, energising place. I immediately talked with about fifteen students, and then saw the accommodation where the GAPpers would go – bare, murky and empty now. I was given a room to sleep in. (The foreigners' building I used on later visits had not been built.)

The all-pervading damp fog swirled in through the windows, the duvet was distinctly damp and I went to bed fully clad in suit and anorak.

The next day began early with loudspeaker music crackling over the campus. I went without a real wash – my shave was mirrorless in a cold shower over the loo-hole. After seeing round the campus, I had an interesting question and answer session with about eighty students, the whole English department. As usual, I was asked the inevitable question about Hong Kong, which Madam Luo tried to disallow, but I insisted on giving my usual diplomatic answer. After lunch Liu Hang and I took to the road again, back to Chengdu. The traffic was even worse. We left at 2 p.m., had a brief supper at Jenyang with the local municipal *jiaowei* and arrived back at the hotel at 9.45 p.m., only to discover that we had missed the headmaster of a Chengdu middle school, No. 22, who had come to see me. (It later became one of our placements.). It had been a very long two-day outing, made far more arduous by Liu Hang's incessant chatter the whole way back.

Nevertheless, the excursion was a great success. I now had a placement not only at Guanghan CAFC, but also one for the more resilient in a remoter part of Sichuan, parallel to, and a suitable substitute for, Yueyang in Hunan, which had sadly ceased in July 1994 due to our inability to bring any Hunan Chinese teachers to the UK. Carehome was due to start in February 1995, but I felt doubtful of it. The next morning, Wednesday, November 9th, on my way to the airport I called in there, had another look, and emphasised the GAPpers' need for challenge. Zou Jia then drove me to the airport, and I flew to Hong Kong, and after a brief visit to the Guangzhou CAAC GAPpers, Jonathan Whittaker and Keith Morgan, flew home to the UK via Singapore.

### The Handover (May 1995)

It was now the late autumn of 1994. I had been appointed project manager as long ago as the spring of 1988 and the project had really got under way in September 1990.

Originally I had sent out a mere six GAPpers each semester and twelve in a full year. I calculated that in February 1995 twenty-eight would go that semester, making a total of fifty-six a year – a substantial, almost fivefold, increase. In addition, there were now nine, not six, Chinese to place in the UK each year. Between 1990 and December 1994 I had located a total of 43 young Chinese in UK schools or colleges each for a year. Nevertheless, placements for them in the UK were still appallingly difficult to find; in fact, the situation was getting worse. This was for me by far the most burdensome part of the whole project. Thanks to the meticulous help given by Chinese authorities, colleges and schools, and to the high quality and conscientiousness of the volunteers, the project was, with one or two exceptions, an undoubted success.

On the other hand I had no wish to preside over a project expanding so rapidly beyond the point where I could know each volunteer as an individual. For me that was essential. Additionally, by the summer of 1995 I would have been project manager nominally for seven years, while the project would have been running fully for five, long enough for most GAP project managers. I consequently asked John Cornell, the GAP Director, if he could look for a successor to take the leading role, while I might continue in a reduced capacity, running perhaps Western China (Sichuan and, possibly later, Yunnan), and the four CAAC colleges (at Guangzhou, Shanghai, Guanghan and, later after 1995, Tianjin). In December 1994 John appointed Michael Potter to take over the "lead" role in China, while I was to continue, as I had hoped, to have responsibility for West China and the CAAC. That was a happy arrangement. Michael and I agreed to go out to China the following May (1995) to look at our own particular placements and then have the official handing-over at a GAP conference in Hangzhou.

I flew out to China again in May 1995. There was still consolidation to do in Sichuan. After seeing the Shanghai CAAC couple, Charles Walker and Nathan Walters, I flew to

Chengdu on May 8th and saw the first two Guanghan GAPpers, Joe Twinn and Greg Mulheirn, working at the Flying College. They had settled well into what was a semi-military environment with uniforms and bugle calls very much in evidence. From there I looked at a replacement for Carehome, which was clearly necessary. Cai Li had suggested No. 22 (Etiquette) School, training girls for the tourist industry. This school, whose headmaster I had missed seeing the previous November, was set in the heart of Chengdu amongst old, half-timbered buildings, picturesque, but probably insalubrious; they were fast being demolished to make way for featureless high-rise flats. The accommodation at the school would be well up to GAP standard, the staff friendly and the challenge, as far as I could see, would be right, and it proved to be so.

The next day I went to see the first two at Neijiang. I travelled there, again with the talkative Liu Hang, though mercifully this time by train. The noise of the train's hooter prevented me from hearing a word of what he was saying, but he still talked. I moved away out of range, and immersed myself in Margaret Thatcher's *Downing Street Years* – I managed to read two chapters on the Falklands War. It was hot and steamy in Neijiang – the temperature was 35C with maximum humidity. That evening I attended a disco in the college hall, and almost dissolved with heat, so much so that I refused every attempt to get me to take to the dance floor! These first two GAPpers had settled in fairly well, though they did not have the quality that we needed for the first in a placement (mistakes they made were set right by their successors). Before leaving the next morning I had a fascinating discussion with some of the college students. They were drawn from some of the most remotely rural parts of Sichuan, and on arrival were usually acutely homesick, so strange was the ambience to them. Eventually they would return to their remote local schools to teach English. One of these, Zhao Jun, who proudly called himself a "peasant", not a farmer, knew some English, but could speak little at the

67

beginning of this term. By the time I arrived he could hold a fluent discussion with me, thanks to daily conversation with our two GAPpers. Here the fabled "ripple" effect of GAPpers' work was at its most potent, its most tangible. These students, once qualified, would return to their localities and teach English for a lifetime in the local middle schools to countless thousands of peasant children, the so-called backbone of China. The eventual impact of GAPpers working, especially in this rural context, would be immeasurable.

The following day in Chengdu, Tan Jun and I visited Carehome, and talked to the two girls, Marina Jamieson and Sarah Best. As I suspected, they were not being given enough work, and felt bored. It was a totally unsatisfactory placement, and I told Zou Jia, the chairman, and Gan, the headmaster, that I would have to terminate the placement at the end of that very semester. There were no hard feelings. Courteously Zou Jia told me he quite understood, and even offered me a free room in his hotel at any time in the future. He himself lifted my cases into the boot of his Cadillac before driving me to the airport. Sichuan was now consolidated. We were to lose Carehome, but we had three other firm placements at Guanghan Flying College, Neijiang Teachers' College and at Chengdu No. 22 Middle School. The outlook was good and secure.

I then flew to Shanghai, and took the train to Hangzhou. We held the GAP conference at the Zhejiang Agricultural University, and I handed over the leading role to Michael Potter. Chen Wenxiang, our first GAP co-coordinator, who did so much for us to get GAP started in 1990, dropped in to see us. He had resigned as vice-director of the *jiaowei* and was now enjoying being back in academic life as president of the Agricultural University. The meeting itself was rewarding; it took a full day, but we had a chance as friends to reminisce together about all the work and fun we had had together over the five years. It was for me the end of an exciting stage in my life. I then took the train back to Shanghai and thence home.

68

# 6. The Placements

## a. Key Middle Schools – and Foreign Language Schools

Where did the volunteers work? The initial three pairs, in 1990, were in Middle Schools, catering for a full age range from ages 12 to 18. All students in these institutions were especially selected, usually by ability; but often by money or influence. If they had either, parents could get their children, otherwise lacking necessary qualifications, into these so called "key" schools where the teaching was more skilled and the students more intelligent. Chinese socialism did not embrace a comprehensive principle, as we supposedly find it in the UK.

In 1990-1991 two of our first three pairs worked in Foreign Language Schools (FLS) – at Hangzhou and Nanjing. (In 1990 there were nine of these schools in the whole of China, but soon several more were to be added.) As their name implies, they were specifically for training students in foreign languages, principally English, though some learned French, German or Japanese. (Russian, ubiquitous before 1960, was still rare.) Nanjing Foreign Language School, founded in 1963 specifically under the aegis of Zhou En Lai, may, in addition, have been a special training ground for a particular type of government cadre. We had to abandon the Hangzhou FLS relatively soon – as we have noted, our volunteers were under-used and consequently felt unneeded; the Zhejiang *jiaowei*, in any case, found better and more challenging work for them elsewhere. Nanjing FLS, on the other hand, remained a placement for at least nine years. This was too long, for again the school had for years employed so-called professional "foreign experts", trained teachers from abroad, and thus the volunteers still felt understretched, and were only given low level work. This remained a constant problem for us, for, despite protestations from me and from the *jiaowei*, the school still managed to cling limpet-like onto the link, so that their own teachers could year by year go to the UK under our auspices.

Undoubtedly the best placements in these early years were the two "key" middle schools, No. 1 and No. 3, in Fuzhou. In 1990 the city still bore all the marks of neglect, so much so that guide books not only mentioned it as a place not worth visiting, but distinctly discouraged travellers from doing so. It certainly bore no resemblance to the great, thriving treaty port of the late nineteenth and early twentieth centuries. This is in itself was a benefit for our young GAPpers, who needed a "real China experience". Both these "key" middle schools had an admirably high entrance level, and for the time, 1990, had ample investment in educational technology, many computers, and even a private radio station. In the 1960s the buildings of No. 1 had been the centre of Red Guard activity. When asked what happened in those years, the headmaster and his deputy pointed to a flight of concrete stairs, "That was our part in the Cultural Revolution." With their own hands they had built them under the eyes of their students. Soon now they were to have magnificent new buildings, including an impressive sports hall and new classroom blocks. The finance for most of this came from old pupils, from the overseas Fujianese diaspora in Taiwan and elsewhere, despite the political differences. Here was a fine example of Deng Xiao Ping's pragmatic dictum, "It does not matter what colour the cat is as long as it catches the mouse".

For us in GAP these Fuzhou schools set a standard, a model, for the future. The Fujian *jiaowei* to its credit gave money for a special conversion of teachers' accommodation in the schools. Unmarried Chinese teachers normally lived in dormitory accommodation with shared WCs and washing facilities, which would have caused problems for our young 18-year olds. Instead the Fujian *jiaowei* arranged for our GAP volunteers to have married quarters, but suitably converted, so they had their own flat entrance, two rooms, shower, WC and cooking facilities. Thus in Fuzhou they lived not in a foreign experts' enclave, as at Nanjing and Hangzhou, but amidst the

Chinese teachers, albeit married ones. This became a vital ingredient of our accommodation policy from then onwards, even much later in Hunan, Sichuan and Yunnan. Nor was their accommodation luxurious, but had a degree of drab discomfort, suitable for a true GAP experience. This indeed was to be the kernel of all future development. Further, the headmaster, Mr. Zhu Ding Feng, and his staff, and Mr. Xie Yong Quan, the deputy head of No. 3, and his staff provided an incredible welcome. This welcome, together with the GAPpers' challenging, hardworking role as class assistant teachers, and their experience of Fuzhou before the 1990s boom swept away the city's dusty, rundown character, all this became the launch-pad for GAP-China. These two Fuzhou schools, which provided such a remarkable experience and model for the future, continued to receive volunteers until at least 1995. Unfortunately for us however, by this time Fuzhou had become yet another pale imitation of Hong Kong, complete with MacDonald's, KFCs, Starbuck's and all that goes with consumerist westernisation. Fuzhou was no longer the true Chinese experience it had at first delivered and for which we still looked.

No. 9 School at Qingdao (from 1991), was another prestigious key middle school, founded in 1910 and which was about to be redesignated a Foreign Language School. It gave us similar experience – with high quality students and good integration with staff. The accommodation problem here was at first rather inadequately solved by using a small room in the No. 29 (tourism) Middle School's practice hotel – The Espero – for our No. 9 GAPpers, in return for some additional teaching at No. 29. This was barely satisfactory; the room was too small, the plumbing leaky, there were no cooking facilities and there was an extremely tight curfew. But despite this problem the Qingdao No.9 placement got off to a good start and lasted until at least 1999. Nevertheless, as we have seen, the headmaster told me years later that the GAP programme did much to improve the standard of English in the school,

71

while at the same time giving our young GAPpers a great experience in a delightful seaside city.

Nanjing Foreign Language School also provided placements all through the decade, but, as we have already noted, its value for us and our volunteers was limited. The students were bright, and therefore challenging, but the most challenging were taught by "foreign experts"; furthermore, our GAPpers had to live in the bungalow style experts' enclosure, the "Dawn Garden", and eat separately there away from the other Chinese teachers. There was little contact with staff or students outside class hours. Their companions were remarkable, but to them quite elderly – a delightful Parisian who taught French, and a warm-hearted Belgian nun, who had lived for many years in Hong Kong, and taught English; both of them were outstandingly kind to all our GAPpers. After two years one of the GAPpers, though still based at the FLS, always taught at Jingling, a former Methodist missionary school in the city centre, but now a "key" middle school. This was a much richer experience, for the school had bright, challenging pupils and no "foreign experts", and our volunteers were treasured. In spite of this, the Jingling GAPper still had to live cocooned in the FLS experts' compound some miles away.

In Shanghai from 1996 onwards our Longhua GAPpers also taught in Jian Jing Experimental School in Changning district of the city. This was an excellent school, and by 1998 the principal, Wu Zi Jian, was keen to have our volunteers there full time. Unfortunately I was unable to make a satisfactory arrangement with the Changning District *jiaowei* before I resigned (1999). In addition, elsewhere in the city these GAPpers from 1997 taught at Min Hang Middle School, a key selective school, founded in 1928, where pupils in the senior three forms were drawn from all over the city, while those in the junior forms were local. It was sad we could not develop these placements.

## b. Zhejiang's Experimentation
## (The Institute of Technology and the College of Traditional Chinese Medicine)

Meanwhile Zhejiang had pioneered another way forward which became the second of our models. Hangzhou FLS, with its lack of challenge and under-use of GAPpers, had clearly failed. Another mistaken experiment followed in 1991-1992 with Zhejiang Institute of Technology. Though the accommodation I inspected in 1991 was suitable, volunteers were again insufficiently used and felt lonely and isolated in a vast campus. The Zhejiang *jiaowei* now, in September 1992, moved our placement for three exciting semesters (a year and a half) to the Hangzhou Traditional Chinese Medical College, founded in 1959, where their task was to teach English to the professors, doctors and lecturers of medicine, not the students. After the total lack of need or challenge in the FLS and the ZIT, here was a genuine task to exercise them. Furthermore, the volunteers lived in the college and integrated superbly with both staff and students. At last we had struck lucky with exactly the right level, provided our GAPpers had sufficient intelligence to cope. Every day they had to prepare a different lesson for the same class. This experience was remarkable and tough, given the fact that all those they taught were highly intelligent medical academics. To see our GAPpers, in particular Libby Gubba and Becky Husband, as I did, teaching them nuances of English language and idiom was fascinating. They did magnificently. But this could only last a brief while, for the principal merely wanted to give her staff a crash course and then cease. For the six volunteers who went there in those three terms the experience had a lasting impact on their lives. One who later took a First in Neuroscience went on to achieve a Cambridge PhD on the effect of the mind on the body; this was directly inspired by Hangzhou placement in touch with traditional Chinese medicine, and the questions it raises.

## Teachers' Colleges

After these three fruitful semesters at the TCM the Zhejiang *jiaowei*'s creative thinking produced another remarkable insight – the use of teachers' colleges. Here they could provide our GAPpers with the challenge they needed, while at the same time directly benefiting the students. These particular colleges had so far never had professional foreign teachers. Not only that, but, even more useful, the students were of the same age as the GAPpers or slightly older, which provided opportunities for integration between the two groups of young people, socialisation outside class time, which would work to their mutual advantage. The GAPpers gained culturally and linguistically from increased contact and friendship with the Chinese and vice versa, something that was impossible in the middle school situation, given the age difference. The Chinese students benefited from increased informal use of English language outside classroom hours, which most professional and older "foreign experts" on longer-term contracts, would be most reluctant to offer. Yet it was these very interactions which were a joy to most short-term GAPpers.

Consequently in May 1991 I visited the Teachers' College at Shaoxing, an ancient Chinese city, famous for producing the rice wine that for centuries had graced the tables of the Imperial Palace in Beijing – and still reportedly makes similar provision for the present Chinese leadership in the Zhongnanhai. The college, newly built on an extensive site, I found to be excellent. The deal was clinched and our first volunteers went there in February 1992. It was a great success, and was followed by others in Zhejiang – Huzhou Teachers' College in January 1994 and Li Shui, taking Shaoxing's place, in the more remote southern Zhejiang in September 1994. As a province, Zhejiang's educational strategy for English teaching was to put GAPpers into these institutions first as the initial foreign teachers, and after two or three years to follow them with older, professional, more experienced teachers, recruited through the Amity organisation. In this way GAPpers never had to follow more experienced teachers, which had been the problem in Hangzhou FLS, and was to continue to be so at Nanjing.

Pioneered by Zhejiang, this use of teachers' colleges became a persuasive selling point in later negotiations in other provinces. After a visit in summer 1993 to Changsha, capital of Hunan, Mao's home province, I was able to establish a placement the following January at Yueyang Teachers' College, far to the north on the shores of the Dongting Lake. This was an immense success. Remote from other GAP placements, it was at that time even remote from Changsha − there was then no motorway, and a journey by rough roads or by rail could take four or five hours. Furthermore, they had little or no experience of foreign teachers. But, though the president always gave me the warmest of welcomes, the *jiaowei* in Changsha remained unhappy, because we failed to initiate a proper exchange for Chinese teachers or even invite a delegation of education officials to the UK. Much to my regret the *jiaowei* terminated the arrangement in July 1994 after only three semesters.

My experience with teachers' colleges in Zhejiang and Hunan led me to recommend these institutions when I reached Sichuan in 1993 and 1994, and I later suggested it in Yunnan, when, as always, I explained our need for a combination of academic challenge and remoteness. The Sichuan *jiaowei*, at first reluctantly, sent me to negotiate with Neijiang Teachers' College. Consequently by February 1995 our first GAPpers were in place at Neijiang. Unhappily because I had had to choose them rather rapidly they were not a great success, but the next pair set a high standard, redeemed the situation and set a pattern for what turned out to be one of the most rewarding, if arduous, placements. Again the Zhejiang model worked well. The volunteers soon developed an excellent rapport with staff and students, who were mostly of farming stock, "the backbone of China". Neijiang was as remote in Sichuan as Yueyang was in Hunan, but in addition most of the students were from rural families – "peasants" as they proudly described themselves. The "ripple" effect was far more pronounced in these teachers' colleges than in middle schools. The young trainees, taught by the GAPpers, would return to rural middle school in deepest Sichuan, and teach English to thousands of the rural Chinese in the many years ahead. Initially the college had had no experience of foreign English teachers, and thus treasured our volunteers. A year later the American Peace Corps arrived, but, though the situation changed a little, their paths did not clash. The Americans, better qualified as they were (they were university graduates), rightly did the more specialised work of teaching students "majoring" in English, while the GAPpers taught those "majoring" in other subjects. (All students, whatever their teaching subject, had to pass English as a core subject. This applied to future teachers in the sciences as much as to those in the humanities.)

## c. Types of Specialist School

As the Chinese economy boomed, particularly on the eastern seaboard, so the demand for specialist education developed, with students designed either for tourism or commerce. As time passed, we were called into more specialist institutions. The first was in 1991 at Qingdao No. 29 School which provided the No. 9 GAPpers with accommodation, and in return the volunteers worked partly in No. 29, teaching future hotel staff of all levels. (This fulfilled a similar function to our Hong Kong project's Kwuntong Vocational School.) Similarly in Chengdu, from 1995 onwards, GAPpers worked in No. 22 (Etiquette) School where the students were in the tourist industry; such as future hotel staff, and air stewardesses. The academic standard of the students in both places was appreciably lower than in the key middle schools, but both provided useful experience for our GAPpers.

At the end of the period of this study in the mid-1990s, as the Chinese economy continued to prosper, a new breed of secondary schools, connected with the business community,

76

began to flourish. These were naturally comparatively flush with money and could afford GAP more easily then the normal government schools, who at first felt unable to have a GAP arrangement without a proper reciprocal exchange programme. Here Jiangsu led the way. In May 1994 I visited schools at Wuxi and Suzhou, the famed "City of Gardens". In Wuxi prospects were good at No. 12 Middle School. At Suzhou, the Professional High School and the delightful Jingfan Garden School were both keen to have GAPpers. The economic boom in Jiangsu had reached such a level and the demand for English language had become so urgent that some schools not only had the money to pay, but were keen to have our volunteers without even mentioning any reciprocal arrangement at all. Hence we began our two placements at Suzhou in the Professional High and Jingfan Schools in September 1994 and at Wuxi No. 12 the following February (1995). There was, however, a disadvantage. For a real GAP experience, placements in poorer, rundown areas were more suitable for our volunteers. These schools were by their very nature in an ambience of burgeoning consumerism, almost Hong Kong-like in many places – and for many this was a pity. Nevertheless, this brief spurt was a prelude to the vast expansion within Jiangsu and Zhejiang under Michael Potter in the years that followed.

## Carehome

One of these specialist establishments was a private, fee-paying school, Chengdu Carehome School, a private institution on the outskirts of Chengdu, where the first GAPpers went in February 1995. The placement here was not a success for various reasons, much as I privately admired and liked the young entrepreneur. One GAPper later described it as "an extremely strange placement" though it was character-building and distilled one's resourcefulness. In May 1995, I ended the arrangement with effect from the end of that term. In its place we had Chengdu No. 22, mentioned above, which was far more successful.

77

### d. CAAC and Rolls Royce - a success story

Rolls Royce, already one of GAP's financial supporters, provided a wholly different and rewarding dimension for us. They had important investments in China, specifically in aero-engineering and power plants. As part of their aero business, they had established a strong relationship with CAAC, the overriding regulatory body for all Chinese airlines, and also with some of the Chinese airlines themselves, particularly China Southern. My GAP-China connection with Rolls-Royce developed at a meeting I had with Brian Evans of Rolls-Royce (he was General Manager of Management Development and Training) at their Filton, Bristol, offices early in 1991.

### Guangzhou Civil Aviation Engineering Academy

The first of our CAAC placements was the Civil Aviation Engineering Academy near Baiyun Airport at Guangzhou, which I negotiated on an unforgettably hot day − 25th May 1991 − during a day-trip from Hong Kong. The Academy's students were trainee technicians who not only had to understand the Rolls Royce engine manuals, but also speak with their foreign counterparts, when maintaining the machinery. As we have already noted, the negotiations were tough; the principal, Lin Guo Liang, held me for two hours on, it seemed, one point; that Chinese teachers should go from his college to the UK as part of the GAP scheme. This I had to resist stubbornly on two counts − not only did his college already sent lecturers to the Rolls Royce headquarters in Derby on a frequent and regular basis, but there was such a dearth of GAP placements available for Chinese in the UK. Despite this memorably long tussle in the heat, all was agreed, and I remember vividly being shown round on the hottest of May days up and down, up and down so many teaching blocks. The first GAPpers went the following September (1991) and their successors were still there when I resigned in June 1999. Lin Guo Liang, despite his tough negotiating stance, became a firm and good friend; as fellow educationists, we saw very much eye to eye. Accommodation here was good and totally satisfied our requirements. Teaching was in large classroom blocks where the noise of planes passing overhead, coming in to land at Baiyun, was all-pervasive; on hot summer days, with classroom windows wide open made conversation, let alone class teaching, difficult. A major problem here was that the students' timetable was so crammed with technical subjects that they had little time for their English. For GAPpers who did not mind being in a large city – and that a Cantonese-speaking one – Guangzhou was good. It was less so for those keen to practise their Mandarin Chinese.

**Shanghai Vocational School of CAAC**

The second CAAC placement was the Vocational School of CAAC at the old Longhua Airport at Shanghai. Guangzhou proved such a success that eighteen months later, while on a regular visit to Shanghai, Rolls Royce invited me there. This airport was famous in World War II as the Japanese internment centre for Shanghai Europeans, and was the ambience of J.G.Ballard's semi-autobiographical book *Empire of the Sun* and its subsequent film. Whereas Guangzhou trained technicians to service the aero-engines, Shanghai was primarily for training potential ground staff (tickets and baggage) and some air-stewardesses. Richard Thorne, Rolls-Royce's head of language training in China, took me to the school. I clearly remember negotiating the GAP agreement with the principal, Zhang Xexian, a delightful man. At last we had a good placement in Shanghai after the unsuccessful attempt with the Jianguo Hotel and the Music Conservatory. The first GAPpers went there in September 1993. The placement continued most successfully until 2000, when the whole arrangement between GAP and Rolls Royce, to my sadness, came to an end.

This Longhua placement was within easy reach of the main shopping areas of Xu Jia Wei and Huai Hai Lu and of the city centre, Renmin Square and the Waitan (Bund). Originally in 1993 when the arrangement started, Longhua was in a rundown state which amply suited the GAP ethos and was much liked by GAPpers, but soon afterwards the whole area was subjected to colossal urban high-rise development; the old air terminal building is now completely engulfed and the runway has virtually disappeared. Pizza Huts and other fast food outlets have replaced the delightful small, simple restaurants; tourist paraphernalia now surrounds the nearby ancient, beautiful Longhua Temple and its pagoda. Old Longhua GAPpers, when they return, are as saddened as I am by this change, much as it has improved the lot of the local Shanghainese.

## Guanghan Civil Aviation Flying College (CAFC)

The third CAAC placement was in Sichuan at the Civil Aviation Flying College at Guanghan, one hour by road from Chengdu. This led directly from our work at Guangzhou and Shanghai. This had been successful enough for CAAC to want us to send GAPpers to a more prestigious place, and in 1994 I went to discuss the project there. Reportedly Guanghan itself had achieved national fame as the district, where Zhao Ziyang and Deng Xiao Ping, a Sichuanese himself, had earlier tried out their economic reforms. The college, a former military air base and perhaps training centre, was set in the countryside amongst sugar cane crops, and yet near Guanghan town. It was a prestigious college of university standing where trainee pilots attended most of a four-year course. It still retained its military ethos enough for the first and second year trainee students to have to wear military-style uniform; in addition, meals and parades were announced by bugle call, redolent of my own teenage military experience. In the third year the students went elsewhere for basic flying training, and returned for the fourth, for the final course towards passing out as fully qualified airline pilots. Our GAPpers taught only the first two years. Though there were female members of staff, including the charming, supportive vice-president,

Madam You, and the head of English, Madam Gong, the college was an all-male student body. This meant that I normally appointed male GAPpers. Our one attempt to send girls was unsuccessful, for the all-male community was daunting, and these two girls advised me against repeating the experiment! The accommodation was excellent, and the relationships good. As in all other CAAC colleges students were drawn from all over China, some came from the far west, Xinjiang or Tibet, some from the far north east, Jiling, some from Shanghai, Yunnan and Guangdong. This in itself was fascinating and educative for our GAPpers. Most were from selective middle schools, but some were already graduates in other subjects from other universities. Some indeed were already experienced airline pilots who had returned to bring their English up to standard for the new CAAC regulations, now demanded even for domestic routes. Our first placement here was in February 1995, but with the other CAAC colleges, the arrangement ended in 2000. It was one of our best Chinese placements.

**Tianjin Civil Aviation Institute of China (CAIC)**

The fourth and last CAAC institution GAP served was the Civil Aviation Institute of China (CAIC) at Binhai Airport, Tianjin. Again of university standard, this was even more prestigious than the last, and indeed in 1999 achieved full university ranking in the Chinese national educational system with the title of the Civil Aviation University of China (CAUC). All of remarkably high calibre and intelligence, the students, again from all over China, were mostly selected as future senior management personnel, interpreters and translators. This was a real challenge for our GAPpers, who had to be quick-witted and nimble-minded with fresh ideas almost daily. Accommodation was excellent – the GAPpers each had a large sitting room and bedroom, and cooking facilities – far more spacious than they would have at home, or certainly at their future UK university. Some found the isolation of being away from the city centre, up near the

81

airport a disadvantage, though they could easily cycle to the city centre. Polluted though Tianjin was, as a former treaty port like Shanghai, it boasted a number of old western-style buildings to interest the historically minded. To be asked to teach at CAIC (CAUC) was a great accolade for our GAPpers, and Professor Qin Qing Sheng, the Vice-President, and Kevin Wu, the Head of Foreign Affairs, much appreciated their work, and wanted us to continue. It was arguably the most academically prestigious placement we had in the years up to 1999. The first volunteers went there in February 1996, but unfortunately with the fall in GAP-China recruitment we were unable to supply any after June 1999, and, as we have seen, the whole connection with CAAC was severed in 2000. This was extremely sad. It was an excellent placement and both CAUC and I were very keen to continue.

# Photographs

**The first two volunteers in Fuzhou. Oct. 1990
(l. to r. Christian Turner and Simon Hughes)**

**Du Jian. GAP co-ordinator on West Lake,
Hangzhou (Oct 1991)**

**Peter Price-Thomas at work in Fuzhou No. 1 School
(Nov 1991)**

**Three GAP agents meet at Fuzhou (Nov. 1991)
(l. to r.) Sui Zhi Qiang, Du Jian and Sun Hai Feng**

**Libby Gubba teaches medical lecturers at Hangzhou (Oct. 1992) p.39**

**Bob Allen holds an English corner at Fuzhou No.1 School (Nov. 1992) p.44**

**Noel Casey at work in Yueyang (Oct. 1993) p.51**

**Du Jian, WMM and Dan Large en route for Li Shui
(Oct 1994) p.62**

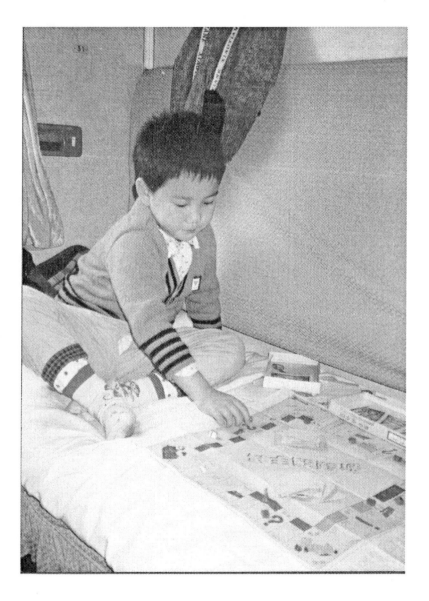

**Chinese Monopoly on a train going to Nanjing
(Oct. 1993) (p.50)**

**The Project Manager takes the lead
near the Dong Ting Lake, Yueyang!**

# 7. The Hong Kong Dimension

Hong Kong, from the first, was bound to be pivotal in all my journeys to China, even though inevitably we had no GAPpers there yet. Until 1997, when it moved to Guangzhou, I had to make regular visits to the UK-South China Consulate-General, based in Hong Kong, and its accompanying British Council office. (Curiously there were then two British Council offices in Hong Kong, one for South China and one for Hong Kong itself.) Fujian province and its capital, Fuzhou, where we had volunteers, fell under the South China consulate's purview. Very soon, as we shall see, I had established a Hong Kong project which itself required regular visits.

But there was, at the start, a more compelling reason – finance. Under the original 1990 GAP Agreement with the Chinese made at Nanjing, GAP itself had to fund the international airfares of the Chinese volunteers to and from the UK (UK GAPpers always paid their own); the Education Commissions claimed not to be wealthy enough yet to pay the cost. In October 1990 I had already asked our Shanghai Consul-General if he thought any Chinese non-state business would help financially. Chinese business indeed stood to benefit directly from better English teaching in schools from Chinese teachers who had been teaching for a year in UK schools. But, unlike in the UK, donating to charities like ours was not then part of Chinese business thinking. I took home to GAP cards of various business enterprises working in China, but initially that bore little direct fruit, apart from Rolls Royce – and later Cable and Wireless.

## First Contacts – the January 1991 visit

The cost of these airfares was to be a constant drain on GAP's resources, unless something was done, and done quickly. By the time I reported to GAP on my return from China in November 1990, John Cornell had already taken action, and had rapidly planned a fund-raising expedition to Hong Kong.

This was to take place almost immediately, inside one week the following January (1991). Five of us went – John, his wife Caroline, his PA Sarah, the Appeal Director Gill Cowell and me as China Project Manager.

At the time the Gulf War was still raging. There were tanks on duty at Gatwick when I left on Sunday, January 20th 1991; and the flight took me the circuitous route over Russia to avoid the Middle East. On this occasion I stayed with a friend in a charming Spanish style villa near Junk Bay. The money raising started at once, and on our first morning, the Tuesday, John, Gill and I had breakfast with David Tang at the Mandarin Hotel. This was our first meeting with the successful, colourful Hong Kong entrepreneur, and he astonished us by offering GAP a generous, substantial sum straightaway. We had made a good start. But it was clear from the beginning that, if we were to attract substantial Hong Kong finance for the mainland China operation, we would have to set up a project in Hong Kong as well. The material poverty of many Hong Kong Chinese and their obvious lack of fluency in English language, so much worse than on the mainland, left us in no doubt about this.

Despite some jolly occasions, such as Tuesday evening's private boat outing to Lamma Island, there was much work to do. The two recent Hangzhou GAPpers, Keri Glenday and Astra Holmes, and I were interviewed on Hong Kong radio the next morning (Wednesday), but it was that afternoon that my work to set up a Hong Kong project really began. A visit to the Government's Education Department proved fruitless. I had expected as warm a welcome as I had had from the mainland Chinese education offices, but it was not so. I gave my usual presentation about GAP, but the Chinese Director of Education and his British deputy gave me a total brush off, which surprised me. It was well known that all business employers in Hong Kong and many others were worried by the poor standard of spoken English amongst their employees, and the root of the problem lay in the schools. English language was supposedly by regulation the teaching medium for all subjects, but, once classroom doors were shut, teachers taught in Cantonese. The Hong Kong government, with British Council help, had tried to introduce native English-speaking teachers into schools, only to be met with a ferocious Chinese backlash; a teachers' strike. When I heard this, I understood the education department's reluctance even to consider GAP schemes in their schools. Apart from one rather useless suggestion of brief work camps in July or August − at the earliest in 1992 – we were up a blind alley. Furthermore, the incentive of sending reciprocals from Hong Kong to the UK cut no ice at all. Taking a gap year was not part of Hong Kong family ethos; school-leavers always moved speedily after school into training, and then work. I vainly pointed out how mainland Chinese education authorities welcomed GAP with open arms, and yet here, in a territory still nominally British, we had a brush off. Though I understood their problem, I left the building feeling chastened.

Later in the week I went to see "Gus" Chui, the Hong Kong Government Secretary for Recreation and Leisure, a member of Exco (the Executive Council), and in effect a government minister. We met in his vast, amply-furnished Harbour Centre conference room with the Queen's official portrait as its centrepiece. Educated at Trinity, Oxford, he was most sympathetic to the idea of a GAP project for Hong Kong, and in our talk for over an hour he clearly disagreed with the education department's caution. Heartening though it was to have his warm acceptance, it did not alter the situation.

That Wednesday evening after my chilly rebuff I was glad temporarily to put my despondency behind me by attending the well-attended fund-raising get-together at Head Quarter House in Barker Road high up on the Peak overlooking the Harbour. This was the official residence of General Peter Duffel, Commander of British Forces, a friend of John Cornell's who had kindly agreed to hold the event there. It was a chance to explain GAP plans and philosophy to senior financiers and other notables of Hong Kong, and ask for their support. The general, John Cornell and Lydia Dunn, a leading Hong Kong figure, all extolled the virtues of GAP, aided by Keri Glenday, the GAPper recently working in Hangzhou, who spoke a few words of mandarin. It was a worthwhile evening.

My attempts to make progress through the most obvious channel, the education department, had been a failure. The second prong proved altogether more successful. The next morning we met Rosanna Tam (now Wong), who coupled membership of Legco (the Legislative Council) with being in charge of many charitable youth activities in Hong Kong. Far from giving us another brush-off, she was distinctly positive. She agreed that youth social work in Hong Kong would not be right for GAP – difference of language loomed too large – she nevertheless suggested we use her Hong Kong Federation of Youth Groups, not for social work, but for teaching and English conversation. The Federation was a network of some 25 youth centres spread all over Hong Kong, especially in the poorest parts. Hong Kong family accommodation was so cramped, often with one family to a room, that the Federation provided these centres not merely as youth clubs with recreation facilities, but with classrooms where teenagers could do their homework for the next day. She suggested that our GAPpers could have a multiple role; not only should they teach some English, but hold informal conversation, and also, perhaps, most importantly, make friends and socialise with the young Hong Kong Chinese who in normal life barely set eyes on a European, let alone spoke with them. With the GAP project, she felt, their English, often very feeble, would improve, and, in addition, the terrible barriers between the poorer Hong Kong Chinese and Europeans would come down. This looked to us a way out of our impasse, a way to start.

Nonetheless, accommodation, extremely costly in Hong Kong, remained a major quandary, and the Federation had no facilities of its own to solve it. We could do little in the short time remaining that January, so we left this problem over for

87

my visit in May. At least now the seeds of the Hong Kong Project had been sown; more placements and a solution to the accommodation question we hoped would follow.

## The Cheshire Home

As part of my China journeying I was to visit Hong Kong twice more in 1991, in May and November. The Hong Kong scheme gradually emerged through these months, though not without its disappointments. Rosanna Tam's Federation of Youth Groups would at most only be able to take two GAPpers. I needed to look further, and, feeling a little desperate, I again briefly enquired into the social sector, despite the language problem. GAP already sent volunteers to Cheshire Homes in, for instance, Japan and Malaysia, so there seemed no harm in trying this field. On May 22nd I visited the Cheshire Home at Shatin, in a beautiful new building with stunning views overlooking the famous racecourse. An official received me warmly and showed me round, but, as the Home was not yet at its full complement, they could give no definite commitment about GAP. Additionally, accommodation, as ever a Hong Kong problem, presented itself again – as usual, it was either too expensive, or too unsafe for young people. On my side I had doubts about young GAPpers working in a Cheshire Home at all; nevertheless, as they did so in other countries, I put my doubts aside. The following November, when I was in Hong Kong again, the idea was killed stone dead. The new Cheshire Home administrator made an appointment to see me, only to tell me abruptly on arrival that they had given up the idea. Here was another blind alley, another rebuff. It was perhaps a mercy in disguise; I doubt if I would have been happy with it.

I also looked into the possibility of our GAPpers helping with evening language classes for secretaries, working in the finance and business community. As I have already noted, businesses were seriously worried by their Chinese secretarial staff's lack of fluency in English, and accordingly I visited Brigadier Ian Christie, Chairman of the Hong Kong Chamber of Commerce, on May 27th. He too was worried, but any plans we discussed foundered yet again over the ubiquitous problem of accommodation. Nothing could happen until that was solved.

## Federation of Youth Groups

Meanwhile, possibilities with the Federation of Youth Groups were looking ever more optimistic, and from this other things followed. On May 23rd 1991 I met Paul Chan, Rosanna's deputy as General Secretary of the Federation of Youth Groups, who proved to be an invaluable component in the new project, a Hong Kong equivalent of Du Jian in China. A graduate in biology, he also had a Master's Degree in social work, to which he felt a strong vocational pull. On that first occasion, for almost five hours – 3 p.m. to 8 p.m. – we toured a vastly diverse range of the Federation's centres from the relatively plush middle-class areas, including Hung Hom, to the roughest deprived locations, such as Kwai Chung. I remember being especially impressed with one particular leader in the toughest centre of all, David Chum. The following Monday I met Paul again, this time with Rosanna Tam and another official, a Mr. Ng Shui Lai, Director of the Hong Kong Christian Service, another charity organisation. He was initially cautious, but said he could find work for GAPpers in a vocational school. Things certainly seemed at last to be crystallizing.

The following November, on my third visit of the year, we put the final touches to the scheme. Paul drove me to three more Youth Centres, one in East Hong Kong, one in Mansion Street near Quarry Bay, and on the following day one at Shatin. But he also he took me to see the Hong Kong Christian Service's Vocational School at Kwuntong, and its principal, David Ng, as promised the previous May. The school principally trained waiters, secretaries and potential employees in the tourist industry, not unlike the No. 29 Middle School in Qingdao. It would be an excellent placement. Paul Chan had also addressed the vexed and apparently insoluble problem of expensive accommodation, and solved it by doing a deal with the YWCA in Man Fuk Road off Waterloo Road in Kowloon. Though this meant GAPpers would have to live almost a hotel-like existence, thus losing their treasured independence, it did enable them to have safe and clean accommodation at a reasonable price, paid by the Federation. The YWCA remained the solution for accommodation for all GAPpers in the next few years, until after I had handed over the project.

Paul Chan had done a great job; we were ready, and could start as soon as possible, in fact, in February, a mere two months away. I would send two volunteers, one to the Federation of Youth Groups and one to the Hong Kong Christian Service Vocational School. Furthermore, Paul agreed to be "GAP agent for Hong Kong", to include overall oversight of all GAPpers even of those outside his own Federation's purview. He was invaluable, as invaluable as Du Jian was, and is, in China.

**The Friends of GAP (China)**

At this stage we felt it important to have another level of moral and influential support for both the China and Hong Kong projects. We needed a small group of prominent Hong Kong business, professional and academic people, who could use their muscle, should we have problems in either China or Hong Kong. It was still early days after Tiananmen. They were to be called the Friends of GAP-China. Friends not so much to provide finance as to supply moral backing to both ventures in China and Hong Kong. Four agreed to fulfil this role − David Tang, the Hong Kong entrepreneur; Ronald Arculli, a business man, member of Legco and much involved with charity in the territory; Simon Murray, a British financier, based in Hong Kong, whose daughter had had a GAP placement in Mexico; and finally David Gilkes, Bursar of the Chinese University at Shatin. (Later Sir Quo Wei Lee, Chairman of Hang Seng Bank and Rosanna Wong (formerly Tam) joined their number.) We met initially in the Red Room

90

of the Hong Kong Club in May. Our second meeting, this time for lunch, was during the November in David Tang's new creation, the China Club at the top of the Old Bank of China building; there all five of us met in the sumptuously appointed clubrooms with club staff resplendent in their Gurkha uniforms. (It was here too in November 1992 I met Simon Winchester to discuss his impending journey to Fuzhou and his proposed *Guardian* article on Bob Allen teaching alone over Christmas.)

So the Hong Kong Project was ready to start the following February, at least for two volunteers. On my return to the UK I quickly found two late applicants to GAP, Archie Hawken and Brett Perkins, who fitted the bill splendidly in their placements, flew out on time, and got to work. This Hong Kong placement was a new venture, so dissimilar from the mainland Chinese project – the crowded, teeming ambience of Hong Kong, the nature of the work, the type and cost of accommodation, the shyness and reticence of the young Hong Kong Chinese which needed to be overcome. Finally, in future we had to be especially careful to get the right volunteers, those for whom GAP work in GAP placements was paramount. More than perhaps anywhere else it was all too easy for the "wrong" candidate to apply, the one drawn by the glitz and glamour of Central and the Peak. In fact, in interviews a candidate's personal knowledge of Hong Kong, or having contacts there, was for me a negative recommendation. But these first two did splendidly in their placements.

**The year 1992**

In 1991 the seeds of the Hong Kong project had been sown. Nineteen ninety-two turned out to be a year of totally unexpected, almost exponential, growth. On my next visit to Hong Kong as part of my China tour in May that year, I saw Archie and Brett at work; Archie in Kwuntong Vocational School, and Brett in the Federation's Youth Centre in Shatin. The Chinese staff and the young Hong Kong Chinese students as well, had fully accepted them. The Chinese students had not only invited them to participate with them in the local dragon boat races on May 5th, they had, even more remarkably, invited them into their tiny, cramped apartments, often with one family to a room, in the high-rise tenement blocks, something westerners are rarely, if ever, invited to do. They had also been invited to a family wedding, also almost unheard of. The barriers between the races were coming down, and my greatest hopes were being realised. It was a magnificent start, for which we owed much to these first two for so splendidly setting the correct pattern and ethos.

## CELL

May 1992 spawned two other possibilities – CELL and Law Ting Pong School. David Tang wanted to discuss CELL as soon as I arrived in Hong Kong on May 21st – as he was about to depart abroad. I went straight to his office in Jardine House, where he unfolded his idea of a Community English Language Lab (CELL), sponsored by the Anglo-Hong Kong Trust and Watson's the Chemists, and run jointly by himself and the British Council. When David Tang as a boy of 14 had arrived in the UK for school, he suffered badly from his poor understanding of English language. He was determined to help other Hong Kong Chinese overcome this problem. CELL's aim was to attract Chinese of all ages and backgrounds for free English language classes in afternoons and evenings. The first of these – he hoped for several – was in an upstairs room, lent by Watson's above their shop in Kennedy Town, a long way off the end of the MTR (the underground), and thus well away from the haunts of westerners. Advertisements were placed in the Hong Kong Chinese press, encouraging Chinese of all ages to come free of charge. After my discussions with him and Tom Buchanan, the British Council Director, we arranged for the first GAPper to start the following September.

In November (1992), two months after he, Richard Wright, arrived, I broke off my usual China visit, at David Tang's request, to attend CELL's official opening by the Prince of Wales on November 7th, with Richard present. Though I had to spend a night in Shenzhen en route, I was delighted to be there for the occasion. The following week after completing my work inside China, I was back again, and visited CELL on an ordinary working evening. Such was the shyness of the average Cantonese speaker that CELL had decided to have a Chinese doorkeeper, not a GAPper or Western colleague, to welcome the newcomers; a *"gweilo"* (foreign) face might deter them from entering. It was good to see CELL in action, and, above all, to watch Richard Wright teaching prepositions to a group of sixteen intensely interested students of all ages and backgrounds – customs officers, middle-aged housewives, music service salesmen, young clerks and so on. It was a fascinating experiment in spreading knowledge of English language.

**Law Ting Pong School**

The second possibility that opened up that May was through an educational charity, and I was taken to see a new girls' school of theirs, called Law Ting Pong, out at Shatin. The GAP project immediately interested them, but they stipulated having girl volunteers only, which was no problem. The placement started the following September (1992), and in November I visited its first two volunteers, Susannah Sherriff and Fiona Brown, and watched them teach. Here was another successful placement, whose reputation would spread and encourage others to ask for GAPpers.

The Hong Kong project now had six volunteers every half-year, all staying at the YWCA – two worked in the Federation of Youth Groups, one in the Christian Service (Kwuntong), one in CELL and two at Law Ting Pong. This was as many as I had had altogether at the start of the mainland China Project in 1990. As I have already noted, that November (1992) I watched all six at work, the two girls at Law Ting Pong, Richard Wright at CELL, Edward Higgs at the Vocational School, and the second pair in the youth centres, Ian Selwyn

Smith at Choi Hung and James Hodges at Hung Hom. All had excellent rapport with the students and were doing well.

*The South China Morning Post* quoted me as saying "I have really been quite staggered at how committed these young people feel to the jobs they are doing". I also noted at the time, "All these young GAPpers feel a real sense of commitment to their work". They had fulfilled my wish of dedicating themselves thoroughly to GAP-China's ideal of breaking down barriers between Chinese and English, making friends, as well as teaching English language, but, on the whole, rarely going after the "glitzy" delights of Central. It was far more difficult than in mainland China to succeed in the Hong Kong ambience where the temptations were so great. The future of the Hong Kong project was assured. At the centre of this success was the remarkable work of Paul Chan and his deputy, Angela; in time they freely gave beyond the call of their normal duties. I also owed much to the British Council under Tom Buchanan.

**Future development**

Further possibilities still, further expansion of GAP-HK, were on the horizon before I left Hong Kong that November. One Sunday I had a long phone call from Evelyn Fergusson about yet another educational charity, and in particular about the Women's Club School. Incredibly, they would want as many as four volunteers every half-year. GAP looked as though it was to expand at rather too rapid a rate. If this addition were fulfilled, there would be at least twenty volunteers a year for Hong Kong alone, without taking into account the 34 already working in China that year, 1993-1994. A grand total of 54 at least, probably more, were more than I wanted to manage. For me to fulfil my role as I wanted, I needed to know each GAPper as an individual. Reluctantly I had to ask GAP for relief. It was then that Richard Edwards joined the scene.

By the following April (1993), I was ready to hand over to him. On Monday, April 19th, I flew in from Changsha in Central China, and the next morning I met Richard and Sandy

Au, Angela's successor, at Tai Po Market. From there we did a circuit of the Hong Kong placements over the next few days. We visited all the venues, watching the GAPpers teaching as we went – Law Ting Pong (Joanna Hickling and Alexis Carne), the Kwuntong Vocational School (Max Schaeffer), CELL (Patrick Humphries) and the Youth Centres at Oi Man (Sam Johnson) and Tsui Lam, near Junk Bay (Richard Parker). We looked at the YWCA accommodation.

I introduced Richard to various officials, including John Chan, Angus Chui's successor as Secretary for Recreation and Leisure; Tom Buchanan, Hong Kong Director of the British Council; David Tang [at the Mandarin for breakfast]; the Xinhua News Agency (in effect, the Chinese government's embassy in Hong Kong) and Ng Shui Lai, Director of the Christian Service, who had been previously so sceptical, but was now positive. On the last day, Friday, April 23rd, we had a useful wind-up chat with Paul Chan and Sandy Au. During the week our eyes were also focussed on the future. On April 21st with Paul Chan and Sandy we met Evelyn Fergusson at the Hong Kong Club for lunch to discuss the Women's School which we visited afterwards. Plans for expansion had been laid.

A highlight of this 1993 visit was the second of three evening events at Head Quarter House, this one on Thursday, April 22nd. (The last was in May 1996 which I also attended.) Without John Cornell there, it was understandably a lower key affair than in 1991, and its aim was to thank Hong Kong people for their support to the China project and to report progress. All six Hong Kong GAP volunteers were there. Our host, John Foley, the general, spoke first, followed by me and then Patrick Humphries, the GAPper at CELL. It was good to see amongst other guests Peter Grout, formerly the British Council's Regional Director at Shanghai, who had done so much to help us get the China project off the ground.

Sunday, April 25th, was my last day in Hong Kong as its project manager. The handover was complete. At Kai Tak Airport that evening to my surprise the four male GAPpers,

Richard Parker, Sam Johnson, Patrick Humphries and Max Schaeffer, had taken the trouble to get there to see me off. For me it was a touching end of my stewardship of the Hong Kong Project. After this I was in the territory each time I visited China over the next six years. There was still much to do there for the China project, but I no longer had any GAP-Hong Kong connection, and for me April 1993 was the end of an era. Under Richard Edwards the Hong Project enlarged and prospered, especially the Chatteris connection.

## 8. The Chinese come to the UK

From the earliest stage of negotiation the GAP agreement with China envisaged an exchange of young people of the two countries. There was, however, an immediate problem – in 1990 young Chinese were not allowed to visit foreign countries before university graduation. Though GAP was already pioneering an exchange of 18-year-olds with other countries, in China's case this was clearly out of the question, and we therefore made a compromise. GAP would welcome young Chinese teachers, already qualified to teach English, provided they had not reached the age of 30. Though stretching our rules to the limit, we were still fulfilling GAP's underlying philosophy of "exchanges for young people". [In this GAP differs from the older established VSO which at one time sent gap-aged people abroad, but had long since abandoned that and now concentrates on recruiting older volunteers, professionally qualified in many fields and much more experienced.]

Our new arrangement for the young Chinese, already fluent in English, would, we anticipated, benefit them personally and their careers, by allowing them to spend a year in the UK, developing their linguistic fluency and absorbing British culture. Furthermore, as with their British counterparts, they would, we hoped, establish lasting friendships across the national divide and thus eliminate false preconceptions of each other. Their role in the UK was principally to teach beginner's Chinese language, but also Chinese culture and, in some cases, Chinese cookery, calligraphy or art. Above all, in those early days when mainland Chinese were rarely seen in the West, each of them would be a "question mark", a source of curiosity and an inspiration for questions in whatever community he or she joined. That was the proposal we took to the Chinese Embassy at our meeting in June 1989, and what John Cornell hammered out in co-operation with the Chinese, when he travelled to Nanjing the following spring.

## The First Group of Six

The first six volunteers were chosen by the three initial participating provinces, and arrived at Gatwick early on 6th September 1990. It was a significant moment. I was there to welcome them with John Cornell, the GAP Director, and the "two professors" from the Embassy. Through contact with the senior immigration officer at Gatwick John had ensured – or thought he had – that immigration would be smooth and quick. It was not to be. Despite all our preparations there was a long hiatus. Later we discovered all the Chinese had been subjected to a severe grilling, and in one case to a medical examination, while we waited interminably outside. It did not seem an auspicious start.

But then through customs they came with smiles on their faces. First, the young man, Wang Yuren, an economics lecturer at Zhejiang Agricultural College, destined to be a good friend of my family. The other Zhejiang volunteer was He Hong, a delightful young teacher from the Hangzhou Foreign Language School. Two from Jiangsu; Fang Fang and Hu Man, came from Nanjing Foreign Language School. The other two, from Fujian, were Wu Cailing from Fuzhou No. 1 Middle School, and Lin Qinqiao from Fuzhou No. 3. Apart from Wang Yuren they were all female and came from schools where we had already sent our UK volunteers the week before. It was a great moment. The greetings over, they were driven off to the Chinese Embassy for a 24-hour rest. The next morning, the Friday, we all met again in the Great Britain-China Centre for a briefing, and in the afternoon the link teachers from their host schools came to fetch them. The latter then had their own consultation, while the Chinese were given a quick whistle-stop tour of Westminster, Whitehall, The Mall, Buckingham Palace and other nearby sites. Then came the moment of truth. The Chinese had to separate from each other and be driven off singly to their different locations, not in pairs as the UK volunteers in China were. It was a difficult moment for them. There were indeed some tears shed.

Before departing for China in October I decided that I must see them all in situ. Though it was still early days to make much of an assessment, it was certainly worth doing. At Millfield, Wang Yuren was settling in well. Primarily an economist and not a linguist, his English was barely fluent enough at the start. Working part-time as I did in the same school, I saw him almost daily and could see he was already well liked by the pupils. He was especially skilled in calligraphy. In Essex, whereas Fang Fang, quietly determined, had found her feet at Colchester Grammar School, Wu Cailing, a more mercurial personality, was clearly less happy at Woodham Ferrers despite the warm welcome she received. The remaining three were fine. I watched He Hong teach at Beaconsfield; she much impressed me, though she had the difficult task of co-ordinating her work in five different schools. Hu Man at Marlborough College was well looked after, her work was already much appreciated and she seemed cheerful. (It was only later that she surprised all of us, both in the UK and Nanjing, by clandestinely marrying one of the Marlborough staff.) Lin Qinqiao, the youngest, at Atlantic College in South Wales not only found the school's broadly stretched international ethos difficult initially, but, for her, the college's geographical remoteness, however beautiful its surroundings, was a problem. Despite their apparent lack of preparation they were a remarkable group, much to be remembered, and better than many of their successors.

**Acclimatization Courses**

In the early stages we realised that their preparation before departure from China was inadequate. Qualified though the Chinese GAPpers were in teaching English in their own middle schools and colleges, it was a very different matter teaching the rudiments of their own language to foreigners; they required new and different skills and perceptions. Furthermore, most of those in the early groups suffered from

99

considerable culture shock, coming into a free and open society from a tightly controlled one, just emerging from its Maoist past. In addition, after the first year (1990-1991) the Chinese authorities by and large chose married women who missed their husbands and children, an added cause of homesickness, and a fatal lack of resilience to face a rather lonely life in a foreign milieu; several of them were consequently unhappy and unproductive in their schools. This was a problem to be addressed fairly rapidly. I made two requests at the 1992 GAP agents' conference in Fuzhou – first, that those chosen should be chosen for their resilience and positive personality as well as their teaching ability. Secondly, I asked for more specific preparation for the year that lay ahead. Accordingly in 1993 Jiangsu arranged a five-day course, led by a Chinese professor, for all nine of them at Nanjing University. I wanted them to get a better idea of how to teach their own language to British beginners. Indeed at first their approach was far too particular, too precise – "practise, practise, practise vowel sounds", which was enough to kill any interest. It took us a long time to get them to employ methods similar to our modern TEFL, such as direct method, using and getting pupils to use simple conversation immediately, thus giving them at the end of the first lesson some sense of achievement; to be able to say "thank you", "please", "goodbye", "how are you?" and other simple expressions.

After the first year, we also established a day course for them at the autumn half term in London at the Great Britain-China Centre in Belgrave Square. There they met together with each other and their link teachers, and sometimes with an Englishman, well versed in teaching Chinese in UK schools. At the same time they could discuss common problems of socialisation, accommodation and so on. After the Friday lunch they went off, socialised and had a weekend in London as a group. The meeting was also a chance, in the afternoon, for link teachers to discuss their mutual problems and methods of hosting their Chinese charges, which was so often not easy. This proved helpful. All host schools in the early 1990s found it unexpectedly and unusually difficult at first; they all had to experience a steep learning curve. Meeting link teachers from other schools was a welcome chance to exchange ideas; those already with some experience of Chinese GAPpers had useful pieces of advice to pass on to newcomers.

**The Second Year 1991-1992**

In the second year, 1991-1992, I had to find an extra three places for the Chinese, nine in all. Zhejiang was sending a third Chinese volunteer as part of its deal to have a second GAP placement at Shaoxing Teachers' College. In addition, because Qingdao city was joining the project and accepting two GAPpers, they rightly requested two reciprocal placements. During my whole tenure as project manager, finding places for Chinese teachers was the most burdensome part of the task. Few schools really wanted a "Chinese experience". In the early 1990s all, except the most avant-garde heads of schools and colleges, were forever telling me that the only Far Eastern language saleable to parents and pupils alike was Japanese. In vain did I try to persuade them that, as visitors to China would affirm, business and trade with China was bound to increase exponentially in the next decade or so. They should look to tomorrow, not today. But all this fell on deaf ears. With a few exceptions schools were obdurate. Only later in the decade, after I had given up responsibility for reciprocals, did the situation improve dramatically; then at last some far-sighted independent schools were prepared to start Chinese language for pupils of 8 years old as an alternative to Latin, French or German. Starting in this way, they would take pupils to GCSE and finally, for some, to 'A' level. But there was little of that spirit in 1990-1995.

In the project's second year, 1991-1992, Essex County still took two Chinese reciprocals, and Millfield and Atlantic College again took one each, while Marlborough and

101

Beaconsfield dropped out. Nevertheless, two valuable new connections were made. One was with Merchiston Castle School, Edinburgh, who took one, which, after a short break, in later years they continued to do by sharing the teacher with George Watson's and St. George's Girls School. The Edinburgh connection proved long lasting. The one other new and valuable addition was The Royal School, Bath, which, in spite of a change in headmistress, continued to be a host for the rest of the decade. An interesting addition was Easthampstead School. David Wright, a science teacher by training, but a sinologist by interest, had pioneered at the school a notable Chinese language unit. About 80 pupils learnt Chinese in the junior forms − always the age of optimum absorption of facts and linguistic data − then about twenty took GCSE, and two or three took 'A' level each year. Though David Wright himself only had a Chinese GAPper for one year, our experience of his scheme was a valuable input for GAP. Here was a fine example of what could be done with Chinese language where there was sufficient enthusiasm and will. It became a valuable selling point for me. Indeed, as we have seen, one or two independent schools found they could follow the same pattern, offering Chinese as a parallel alternative to Latin, French or German at primary age from the age of 8, and then throughout the school. I could now show potential host schools what could be done, given the will.

Another addition that year was Downe House, Newbury, the prestigious girl's public school. If I had been able to provide the right volunteer, this would have been an excellent ongoing placement, and I am sure we would have been retained. Sadly, the girl appointed here lacked any resilience or self-confidence at all, and she felt lonely in the remote countryside with no adequate public transport. Consequently she failed to provide any inspiring teaching, and, despite warm-hearted hospitality and valiant attempts by the school, the placement understandably ended after one year. I was sad we finished at this well-known school on such a negative note.

Another volunteer wrongly placed that year, though she was much more resilient, was Jia Aibing, a lecturer at Shaoxing Teachers' College. As she was the last to be chosen, I had to give her the final vacant place. This, it so happened, was at St. Faith's Cambridge, another prestigious institution, but a boys' preparatory school. This turned out to be the greatest mismatch of all, and I should have expected it. Here was Jia Aibing, a lecturer in tertiary education, used to students aged between 18 and 21, pitched amongst primary-age children. When I visited her later in the first term I was appalled to find that she was not even teaching the bright 11, 12 and 13 year olds, but mother-minding those aged 6 and 7 – hardly suited to her professional tertiary teaching career. But she never moaned and responded well. To be fair the headmaster understood the mismatch, despite declaring rather unimaginatively that there was no call for Chinese teaching amongst the 12 year olds. Having myself at one time taught that age group, I knew that bright ones of that age would leap at it. Nevertheless, Jia Aibing enjoyed life in an ancient university city, and her headmaster gave her contact with Joseph Needham, the Olympian figure and one of the most distinguished British sinologists of his day. Then in his 90s, formerly a professor of Biochemistry and master of Gonville and Caius College, Cambridge, he had on retirement turned his mind to the history of Chinese science, set up the Needham Research Institute in Cambridge, of which he was director, and, amongst many other writings, had embarked on his magisterial seven-part *Science and Civilisation in China.* He employed her in cataloguing and sorting his library and manuscripts. He was a fine contact for her.

**Tertiary Colleges 1992-1993**

1992/93 and 1993/94 was the brief period of tertiary college involvement. Newly hived off from local authority control, these former Technical and FE colleges felt they were breathing a new air of freedom – mistakenly, as it turned out. Principals were keen to be adventurous, and quickly showed interest in Chinese studies. Consequently in 1992/93 I was able to get Chinese teachers placements in five colleges as diverse as Henley-on-Thames, Accrington (and Rossendale), Derby, Pontypool and The Wirral. Their geographical diversity was remarkable. Henley is in the plush commuter belt of southern Oxfordshire, Pontypool in the Welsh hills, Derby in the industrial Midlands, The Wirral on Merseyside, and Accrington on the northern edge of industrial Lancashire. All these, except one, were financially able to take a volunteer without sharing with another institution – they were able to accommodate them, often in B&B's, and they could give them enough work to do. This was an excellent way forward; apart from the teaching, the Chinese met the ethnic diversity of our population for the first time. The only tertiary college that felt obliged to share its Chinese teacher was Pontypool; we made an arrangement for it to share with Haberdashers', a well-known girls' boarding school on the outskirts of Monmouth. For Lin Feng, the volunteer, this was an interesting juxtaposition, but the travelling distance between the two was formidable without private transport.

**Increasing Difficulties 1993-1995**

By the summer of 1993, however, the writing was on the wall. These new colleges were not as financially independent as they had first imagined. Pontypool and Accrington, for a start, felt obliged to withdraw. In their place I found only Peterlee, another tertiary college, in east County Durham, a desolate spot for a Chinese teacher, especially with the Geordie accent to cope with. In my last year in charge of the Chinese volunteers, 1994-1995, the situation became even more desperate. I still had to find nine places. Essex continued to take two, the Edinburgh group, Derby, and Royal School, Bath, still had one each. Peterlee dropped out to be replaced by its sister County Durham college, Monkwearmouth. I still had three places to find, and the situation could not have been

104

worse. I searched around vigorously, including, I remember, a college at Wisbech who initially showed some interest, which, however, soon faded. Eventually I had to agree to a Further Education College for the handicapped; the Nash FE Centre in Bromley, Kent, who would take two. I hesitated. As a college for the handicapped, this would be a tall order, hardly suitable for UK young people, let alone foreigners, even for the most resilient of young Chinese. I faxed to China to ask what the chosen volunteers felt. So keen were they to come to the UK that the answers were more positive than I dared to hope, despite the warnings I gave them. In the event, considering the extreme difficulties they had to face, they performed remarkably well. At least at weekends they could get to know London well, which they did.

I had found places for eight. There was still one to find. The ninth Chinese volunteer was Lao Jing from Hangzhou. We had known her for some time. As director of the *waiban* at the Hangzhou Traditional Medical College, she had masterminded and cared for the young UK GAPpers who taught there for three semesters. Now she wanted to come herself. She was no teacher, but a nurse by training. I looked desperately around. Eventually I found something, which was barely suitable, but riskily just possible. I discovered a nursing home for the elderly in Yeovil, Somerset, one that I knew quite well. She agreed to that – unwisely in my view, and I was proved right. My last place was filled. At least I had given the Chinese authorities what they wanted in the game of reciprocity, a place in the UK for each of their volunteers to set against each pair of ours. Nevertheless, in almost every other way this last choice was unsatisfactory. Homes for the elderly were never part of the GAP programme, and, in the end, nobody was satisfied with it. Lao Jing never settled, and was unhappy – the British elderly were too heavy for her to heave about; in the end the nursing home also was unhappy She left early.

It was a catastrophic year for the reciprocal side of the project. Despite my prodigious attempts to find enough suitable places in the UK, and much spent energy, and despite the much-improved calibre of Chinese volunteers I had failed. The weakness of several of our earlier Chinese, in 1991-1992 and 1992-1993 (it improved later), had undermined GAP's reputation and credibility with more traditional schools as a supplier of Chinese GAPpers. In this way we lost such valuable placements as Downe House, Millfield and Atlantic College. It was with a sense of relief that I handed over the poisoned chalice to my successor, Michael Potter. By dint of his own particular energy, skills and contacts, and through a sudden sea-change in attitudes of school heads towards Chinese language, he managed to restore the good prospects we had enjoyed in the first two years, 1990-1992. The reciprocal side of GAP (China) now had a good future.

**Overall Assessment 1990-1995**

Forty-two Chinese volunteers came to the UK in this early GAP (China) period (1990-1995). They varied enormously in their skills and self-confidence, and thus in their resilience in the face of seemingly daunting situations. Nevertheless they gave much to the colleges and schools where they worked. Some of their former UK pupils, later studying advanced Chinese academically, had their early initiation through them; others learnt the rudiments of Chinese language and culture from them, and yet others had their curiosity awoken, in some cases enough to apply to go to China with GAP themselves. For the schools themselves, despite the temporary headaches caused in looking after these young Chinese, it was an enriching experience.

But what of the Chinese themselves? Despite some misgivings at the time, all were grateful for the year in the UK that they had so eagerly sought after. One has written "My understanding of English as a language backed with a rich tradition of culture has been greatly improved − and it has helped my position as a teacher in the college". Another, once a medical lecturer in a Chinese medical college, has written how much it improved her career. Initially, on her return to

China colleague lecturers and doctors often employed her for translating foreign medical articles. But later, on the strength of her year in the UK, she has become an auditor in an assessment company which sets up management systems. Further, because of her time in the UK she was sent by the firm to Malaysia for three months to monitor systems. She was much impressed by the beauty of the UK countryside, "I have never seen such beautiful green hills... The college is located on a hill and (each day) I walked along (the road) treading on gold leaves every day". One in Scotland wrote, "I had a very warm and colourful year... The most important thing is not the beauty of the landscape or the exotic customs to me, nor the chance to improve my proficiency in English (yes, both of these items I have enjoyed), but the chance to make very good friends there, to feel the warmth of friendship when I first arrived in a totally strange place, and to understand that, in spite of all the differences, the people in another culture may be far more close to us than we may have imagined". "The GAP year experience has not only made me a better English teacher, but also introduced into me something unique. I think it is the love of life..."

## 9. Reaction of the UK GAPpers

### a. Instant Reactions

How did the volunteers react to their experiences in this early period 1990-1995? What impression did the experiences make on them? Answers to these questions still lie hidden in the copious diaries they wrote, which many one day hope to edit and publish or use as a basis for novel-writing. Nevertheless, judging from letters sent back to the UK during the weeks in their placements, by and large they had reacted extremely favourably. Statements such as "the most fantastic experience of one's life", "the experience of a lifetime", "great memories" and "you'll love it" frequent the pages. Naturally, however, reactions varied according to the individual personality, the placement itself and the city.

Most went to Shanghai at least once while in China. In fact, for the first three years GAP made mandatory a visit to the Shanghai Consulate-General and British Council after six weeks, this despite Fuzhou in Fujian and Yueyang in Hunan being outside its consular jurisdiction. One of the first groups of six volunteers in 1990 wrote:

"Shanghai itself is a huge and puzzling city. The bund, or sea front, smacks of former decadence and the height of colonialism in the 1930s. It is a different world to the China of Fuzhou – materialistic. The people all wear make-up, jeans, minis, the kids all in the latest fashions (which are everywhere) and department stores with goods that would not be lost in New York, Paris or London. We could buy anything there, although at great expense. We burned a month's wages in a week largely on travel and accommodation... It was like a relax (sic) returning to the west for a little refresh..." "We visited the sights, including the impressive circus, and took a day trip to Suzhou. This was beautiful, but not a Venice of the East. It did however have lovely peaceful gardens, glamorous women and we managed to buy two huge scroll paintings for about 35 kwai (about £4). We saw snakes killed and prepared

108

in the market and everyone guessed our ages at about 23/24". Everywhere the quantity of bicycles made a great impact. In Nanjing for instance, one volunteer soon after arrival reported to her successor that the rush hour "will be the largest assault on your senses ever". The poorest part of Nanjing made its early impact on one of the GAPpers: "Full of cramped, one-room houses with no windows. Women were sleeping on their doorsteps, there were children with running noses and the family chickens roamed the streets. I had never seen anything like it before".

Shaoxing in Zhejiang, on the other hand, was "a very small city, but beautiful, full of character and charm. Sally and I made our radio debut on Voice of Shaoxing". Yueyang in Hunan was also off the beaten track. "Yueyang is not on the normal tourist route, so don't expect too much. Around the college the main thing is the landscape. The college is surrounded by a lake, and low rolling hills, and you can spend a lot of time simply exploring the local area. Behind the college you will find lots of tracks that lead you into endless paddy fields. We took up running just so we could have a good look round in less time... Very near the college (at Yueyang) ... if you walk three miles in a roughly SE direction, you very rapidly find yourself surrounded by paddy fields, small mountains and some excellent rural scenery, complete with grazing yaks and large flocks of strange birds".

Nevertheless, later Yueyang GAPpers resorted to chess and bridge. "Yueyang is very quiet indeed – not a lot happens here. The students are very friendly indeed and their standard of English advanced". "Other than musing over chess boards and novels I have taken up Chinese art and regular sketching to while away the time which again can easily be organised through your students". Another diversion was to be filmed for local television. "We appeared in an advert for a local factory. So, dressed as normal British students, we appeared as two foreign businessmen striking a deal with a factory boss. We talked business, us in fluent English, and he in fluent Chinese, and tried desperately to keep straight faces..."

The Yueyang volunteers, writing to their successors, concluded: "You should have a fantastic time but when rice gets too much, just think of us tucking into steak and chips back home".

Another wrote from Sichuan, "Neijiang (and Tong Xin Ba) is a fascinating place; I think I have been lucky to have spent our time here. It doesn't have the bright lights and western luxuries of Chengdu, but it has a certain something, as you will find out". "Having said all this, Tong Xin Ba (the villagey place), west of Neijiang is nothing whatever like home. I don't see many buffalo wandering past my window in Manor Way. I've just about adjusted to being a minor celebrity; we'll be wondering why there aren't crowds around the streets when we get home … as we leave the flat we're stared at, greeted with shouts of Hi! Hi!, chased by gaggles of Chinese kids and engaged in impromptu English lessons. This is all quite fun really, and is a very good way of picking up Chinese… The welcome here has been truly amazing … everyone is incredibly friendly, a nice change from Beijing where foreigners are mostly treated with embarrassed indifference".

**Conditions and Shortages.**

In the early years GAPpers sometimes enjoyed being without all the comforts of western life. Two early Fuzhou volunteers wrote: "We met up with the others and we (were) so glad we were not in Nanjing/Hangzhou! They are living in foreign teachers' compounds and socialising entirely with foreigners. We felt they might as well be in the UK..." There were certainly shortages in the early days. In 1990 GAPpers in Fuzhou needed batteries, coffee, and a tin mug for a drink; there was also then no access to photocopiers. One complained of his difficulty in buying shaving gear. Chocolate was another item often requested, even as late as February 1993; and batteries, Pritt-Sticks and sellotape were still recommended items to bring from the UK.

**Travel**

One of the Fuzhou volunteers described his return to Fuzhou thus: "We travelled to Fuzhou back on the ferry, a mist-riven junk, crammed full of the obligatory staring, gobbing, smoking Chinese. Some of the younger ones trap you with gestures and say hello. It took 28 hours and the tying up procedure was quite astonishing. And we, in a funny way, were really glad to be back (in Fuzhou)." Later another volunteer took the boat in the opposite direction from Fuzhou to Shanghai for the consulate meeting: "The boat to Shanghai left Mawei (Horse's tail), the port of Fuzhou, at 10 a.m. on Wednesday ... it was like a cross-channel ferry. We had a room for three other men and three women and slept in bunks. It was pretty misty... Shanghai was pretty incredible up the river − huge ships, steaming out and in for miles and miles and miles − massive docks, derricks, wharf factories − giant great wide river... The water was a brownish, milky chocolate colour. We docked at a wharf ... it was raining quite hard ... luckily I had my coat! (On the way to the Pujiang Hotel) we met the first non-Chinese faces for a long time − two American blacks. 'Where are you guys from?' they yelled.

111

We answered and walked off. There was no room at the Pujiang. By now it was getting dark and still raining. We walked back to the seaman's bar and spoke to a Panamanian sailor and had a mutually pointless conversation. Then we all shook hands and went away."

Rail travel could also make impressions. "The train back (from Suzhou) was quite a different experience. Unfortunately our Chinese wasn't quite up to reserving seats. The result was no place on our train along with 50 Chinese! After an initial minor panic we were herded into a queue for the slow night-train – when it arrived I learnt the definition of mayhem! They only opened two doors and there were about 500 people trying to get on instantaneously – and when it comes to competition the Chinese have <u>no scruples</u>! Our disadvantage was our height, because the system is to grab onto the person in front to get forward – we each had people latch onto our necks, which created rather a peculiar sensation. Once I got to the doorway I discovered that indirectly I had half the crowd pulling my rucksack to get on in two pieces! Once we were moving people became much more civilised and one guy even let me share his seat for part of the way. I actually really enjoyed the journey because it gave me a chance to watch the Chinese when they weren't on their best behaviour for me – fascinating! I had a great conversation with the baby just by me – it gurgled back very happily!"

Cycling in cities was also unusual for new GAPpers; most lived within the school or college campus, but some had to cycle. In Nanjing, for instance, where one of the volunteers taught at Jingling (No. 10 Middle School), she had to cycle every day. "The funniest thing about teaching is getting to my school – it must be about 1 1/2 miles and I get there on an old, dodgy, man's bike that I was left. The Chinese think I am <u>really</u> strange as I contort myself over the cross bar in a knee length skirt, size 8 DMS with white scarred moggy-bitten legs! The only way I can describe the experience is like trying to walk against the crowd in the Central London rush hour. It suits my personality brilliantly – you <u>never</u> look

112

behind you (you cannot avoid people, so it is safer to launch yourself off and let them avoid you!) – and as for crossroads … (there) is a medley of trucks, buses, bikes and pedestrians going in four directions battling for priority in the centre... The good thing is that even if you have an accident you aren't going fast enough to do any real damage."

Later, after they had completed their GAP placements, most travelled around for a few weeks, and a significant percentage for many months. By this time, compared with the early days, they were much more adventurous, having gained the necessary confidence and some command of the language. "Hitchhiking", wrote one "is one of the best and worst forms of travel. It's certainly the cheapest. Just keep (the driver) topped up with American cigarettes, then offer to take a photo of him, perhaps with you in it, ask for his address and send it to him later. Usually they don't ask for any money. They'll ask beforehand if they do… Unlike in a bus, you can ask the driver to stop occasionally for photos".

**Other foreigners**

In 1990 at Fuzhou there were a mere twenty foreigners, and these were "largely Yanks, and we have found them a really nice, if elderly, crowd – it is not exactly the nightlife hotspot". Two years later, in 1992, there were still only twenty in all at Fuzhou. In Nanjing in the early years there were over a hundred foreign students (US, German and African). "This has led to a lot of western meeting places such as a couple of very good restaurants, a bar, and a party on Saturday nights".

**Resilience**

Most, even the most sturdy, found the early weeks taxing. "Never quit" was the advice of one. "China is brilliant. In the second week I was near quitting and really homesick … no matter how resilient you are the first weeks are tough. This was my first time I have been homesick (in all my boarding school time since age 11). Just stick it out and it will be really the experience of a lifetime". Another wrote words of dubious encouragement: "We survived. One last suggestion; by all means, any way, whatever reprehensible, keep yourselves happy in China". At Yueyang in Hunan, one of GAP's more remote placements, however, they were able to report: "We can honestly say that we have not missed home at all and settling in was quick, easy, and enjoyable – especially with the help of (the college president and his wife)... As Dan said, Peter, the *waiban* official, is very useful. Good luck. It would be a huge loss if we were the last to be fortunate enough to stay here".

**Health**

Pollution was frequently a trouble. "The pollution, the viruses and chalk dust will get to you, so bring some dust free chalk if you can ... loads of cough sweets, throat lozenges, decongestants". But weariness was often the major problem, sometimes caused in unexpected ways. "(In Nanjing) I think part of the reason that I find teaching hard is because I'm generally quite tired. Healthwise I am fine. But it's just the case of being in a totally strange environment, having no grasp of the language, doing a totally new job and being polite all the time! The most tiring thing here is being polite. At school I'm escorted everywhere by teachers – even to my bike at the end of the day! My head of department (group leader) washes up my lunch things for me etc! It's exhausting! It's also hard, as their grasp of spoken English is appalling – many of Laura's students speak better English than the staff at No. 10 School, so they are all using me to practise on. It's great to be able to come back to the FLS in the evenings and veg!..."

**School and pupils**

Invariably, however, it was the students that were the saving grace. "The teaching has gone very well. We count our blessings that we are with creative, intelligent kids who enjoy our wackiness and humour". At Yueyang the teachers printed a dialogue book for teaching purposes; here in the

114

conversation piece GAP itself and its project manager appeared, as follows:

"LESSON TWENTY-SEVEN - Introductions
1. Dialogues.
A Dialogue with Dr. Marshall.
(Yang Ying is accompanying Dr. Marshall, an English language linguist, to an office. They enter the room.)
YANG − Dr. Marshall, I'd like to introduce you to Mr. Wang, the President of the University. (To Mr Wang) This is Dr. Marshall, an English language linguist.
MARSHALL − How do you do Mr Wang?
WANG − How do you do? Dr. Marshall. We're glad you could come.
MARSHALL − I am certainly glad to be here; I've heard many of the teachers and students are excellent and promising in your university.
WANG − Thank you for your compliments. Some of our teachers and students are quite good. I'm proud of them. But they still have much to learn."

Nevertheless, in at least one teachers' college, motivation was at its most ambivalent. At Yueyang the students …"can be quite negative about any activity that doesn't fit in with what they are learning as trainee teachers. It is worth noting that for most students, teachers' college is second best choice, so motivation is not at a peak. Endless enthusiasm on your part can help a great deal with this problem". At Yueyang again it was reported later that students can, nevertheless, be a godsend. "They are absolute lifesavers, if you take a rather mercenary view of them; they help you with most things − getting tickets, cooking (though a couple wreaked havoc with our pots and pans) and buying food, knowing the right food prices…" "The college … is (for them) a last choice establishment… 'Learn to be a teacher, or get out into the fields and gather hay', is the option most of the students here were faced with, so motivation is not at a premium".

At Fuzhou within the first three or four weeks of the first GAPpers' arrival in 1990, "a huge pile of university students have befriended us – we played tennis today, may go swimming tomorrow and attend one English corner a week on Friday evenings. This is not for the faint-hearted – gassing away for two to three hours being the sole attention of up to 40 crammed in around you... They are so friendly and kind; we go there for a "dance" every Saturday night. Last night the peak embarrassment came, when we were made to disco dance alone on the floor of the hall in front of about 250 curious and amazed students".

In most places they were well looked after, "Thursday was National Teachers Day, where traditionally, all the students give their teachers presents and tell them how wonderful they are. I hadn't started teaching, but Laura got two bunches of flowers and some balloons from her classes today! In the evening the HM, Mr. Xu (Head of Foreign Affairs - i.e. us) and Mr. Dong (Head of Foreign Languages) took all of us foreign teachers out for a meal – unfortunately, a local new 5-star restaurant had heard of this occasion and, as a promotional event, gave us an all expenses paid banquet – it was obscene – the starter was made of 8 little dishes of various things, surrounding a vast plate (two feet in diameter) containing flowers made of fruit and veg and meat. It was incredible. There was a rose made from radishes amongst many others – I can't just describe it; it must have taken one chef all afternoon to prepare. This was followed by shrimps as I've never seen – about 6 inches long on cocktail sticks. The menu was then as follows; baked 10 inch shrimps in batter, Peking duck, mussels, lotus roots, scrambled egg and spinach, bananas in herrings, a cake especially made for us and finally, duck soup with little egg white ducks floating on the top. These are now sitting in our room as we were presented with them as the youngest members of the group! During the whole meal the manager was eating with us – he was obscene – fat, greasy, with manicured long fingernails and he drank and smoked continuously all evening. This is the other end of

116

China where you've got men who can easily afford hi-fi music systems, being sold for Y48,000 ((£4,000), whereas the people are working with a fortnight's salary on a bad walkman – and this is communism!"

## The Chinese

"Above all, it is the people of China that will leave you with the greatest impression, but be prepared to accept the five S's – Spitting, Shouting, Shoving, Staring and Smoking. The cities are overcrowded and there are bicycles everywhere – in rural areas the staring becomes even more common (if this is possible) and you'll have to get used to 'Hello' 'Hi!' 'How are you?' 'OK?' shouted from the passing cars, upstairs windows and everywhere else, wherever you go". Street scenes were sometimes memorable, if typical. "The food here thankfully is still good. I visited the food market by mistake – and what a mistake it was! There are trays of baby lobsters which the owners catch, as they make a bid for freedom. There are crates of chickens and ducks that make battery farms look like a holiday home – there are trays of things we would spray insecticide on, writhing around… And today in the middle of the pavement there was a man picking snakes out of a wriggling bag and putting them alive on the pavement! This is not a place for animal activists! Fortunately by the time Xiao Li has done whatever he does to our meat it is unrecognisable – and with a smile like his he could serve anything".

## Post and telephone/ communications with the UK

With difficult international telephone and fax communications, and before the days of e-mail, communications with home could be wearisome. "The post is slow – on average 10 days, 6 if you are lucky, 14 if you are not. Letters are often opened or go missing completely". Telephones could be difficult. "Best way is to find a hotel, and get parents to ring in at a prearranged time" (1990). At Yueyang, "No photocopy use here. Telephone very expensive and difficult. A good way to communicate with home is to use a fax in the town."

**General Comment**

One wrote soon after her return home, "The real experience offered by a placement is learning how to cope with yourself. Everyone has different experiences, but we all learnt a hell of a lot and came home more mature and confident... There's an amazing sense of achievement when a really shy student comes up and actually speaks to you without any prompting. For all you give in effort and time, there's twice as much given back in friendship and support from your pupils and friends that you make in six months".

One former Fuzhou GAPper, much later a graduate in both Chinese and Japanese, studied at Wuhan University a year after his GAP placement. Once there his changed perception is noticeable. "The anti-foreign feeling is much stronger here and the authorities seem a lot more conservative than their Fuzhou counterparts. I have only discovered this by searching for it, speaking to people, reading and coming into conflict with some leaders of the university by being too friendly to Chinese students. In Fuzhou they trusted us, and we didn't break that trust. In Wuhan they don't trust us. In this respect GAP is wonderful. We get to experience a genuine dose of China, with bias, history and politics all put to one side. I think this was because we on the GAP 91 project had a fondness for China and jumped at the opportunity to live in the country for six months, but we didn't (I know I didn't) really know much about China... ...As the Chinese would say, we were "pure". I would say 'blissfully ignorant'. I wouldn't say that I am still "pure"! So then we were relatively safe, as far as the Chinese were concerned, to teach children, make friends and integrate with Chinese life. This way GAP teachers are very lucky, and it was because of my experience in Fuzhou that I swapped to Chinese (for university). The Chinese here treat all foreign students as unsafe (probably quite accurately) and keep a close eye on us…"

## b. Views from a decade later (2001-2002)

Of over fifty volunteers who, a decade later, replied to a survey, nearly all still spoke favourably of the GAP experience, but for some it was viewed as experience achieved rather than one of real enjoyment. They were now no longer young pre-university students, but men and women who had already started to make their way up the ladders of life. Two were in the Cabinet Office, three in the FCO, at least four were engineers, five in medicine, eleven in business, eight in finance, four in law, two in charity organisations and there were two academics, one a university lecturer in law. At least seven were married; three to Chinese whom they met on their assignment, another to an American Chinese, another still has a Chinese girlfriend from ten years ago. In our first year, 1990/1991, at least two of the five Chinese women volunteers in the UK married British teachers, one even clandestinely in the UK, the other after returning to China.

## Hardship, negative feelings

Looking back over a decade some remembered GAP-China with relish, others however with pain. "I look back quite fondly now", wrote one. "I am always amazed how I got through it. I generally only contain the positive memories – and even the old negatives are now positive. No real regrets now, in fact, I often refer back to my time in China to encourage myself to start shaking up what I currently do in an attempt to get out of my current rut". Later he ruminated that "18 years old in a place like that was a bit of a tall order/stretch. And I continue to have no real respect for GAP apart from the opportunity it presents. I think one of the greatest frustrations, looking back, is never really being able to share the experiences with anyone – quite a lonely memory... I have never really entertained a prolonged return due to some of the "loneliness and exclusion" I think we all felt". A later volunteer also combined this lack of enjoyment with the positive benefit: "I found China very difficult to cope with at times, and, having been there for six months I felt it was a challenge I had to overcome rather than an enjoyable time − but I think that was the spirit I decided to go in to start with". Another philosophised, "…I did not have much of a happy time … but happiness can hardly rate as the ultimate propriety in an interesting and challenging life… Perhaps the most profound effect of my time was that my belief in humanism, and concept of rationality was strenuously tested in a very concrete way rather than merely as an intellectual exercise". During a visit to a traditional Chinese medical hospital, one volunteer, daughter of two English medical doctors, imbued with the principles of western medicine, found her ideas profoundly challenged by a Qi Gong master who to her great surprise cured her loss of voice instantly. For a very few the GAP period made a profound political impact, an intensely hostile reaction: "China, aged 18, in '91 made me hate communism, distrust everyone in China, as Chinese families couldn't even trust each other… I still remain totally suspicious of the Chinese government with their ability to lie to their nation… I believe that my experience in China created a need to see other cultures, to find a 'belief in humanity', to find somewhere nearer Eden, having experienced somewhere miles from it, and thus I have travelled and lived abroad (since) for 28 months minimum".

Most wanted to return, and many did so often for work, for further study as part of a university course in the UK, for post-graduate study or merely for social reasons and to try to relive the experience. One wrote that she hoped to get back soon through her work. "…After drifting away from my China experience (via Japan … and Tanzania, working last year on a development project [with a leading engineering firm]) there may be some opportunities opening up for me in Beijing. We have been working on some of the Olympic infrastructure bids, and I will try to get involved with these which could lead to a job out there". Several however, never wish to return.

Because of this China experience, one was recently given the chance of working there by his multi-national company "to kick-start some business there. The people who approached me did so, as they are aware of my GAP placement – but it is precisely for this reason that I do not wish to return!" More usually, the desire not to return results from the impossibility of recreating the situation they were in. "Curiously I'm not that keen to go back to China. I don't have the innocence of an 18 year old, and I think I would be disappointed to find the intensity of the experience reduced. Plus I believe it has changed dramatically". An early volunteer who gained so much from his placement "never returned to China, always shied away from going back, given (the) inability to recreate (the) experience of (the) placement".

**Great influence on career**

For many, GAP-China had shaped their careers and even their lives. For one in particular, now a programme manager for World Teach based in Cambridge, Massachusetts, USA, when asked if GAP had influenced her work, replied "Very much so. Fundamentally." One of the programmes she runs is in Yantai city, Shandong, though she is also responsible for programmes in Ecuador, Namibia and Costa Rica. "My interest in the job and organisation is related to my own transformative year as a GAP volunteer, and it is rewarding to work to give others a similar opportunity, as well as make some impact on international education and development." For another "GAP changed my whole life (without any exaggeration). It opened my eyes to a whole new overseas world." She read PPP (Psychology, Philosophy and Physiology) at Oxford, followed by an MSc in Medical Anthropology, was a research assistant in Vietnam and Tanzania and then worked for a year as Save the Children HIV/AIDS Adviser in Malawi; she now works in the Social Exclusion Unit in the Cabinet Office. Another, after leaving the army spent a year working on an AIDS programme in Ghana, largely because of his GAP experience. One former

121

GAPper, now a diplomat overseas, a second-secretary, when asked whether GAP had influenced his career, replied "Completely. I decided to seek work experience... I considered China a key part of what made me individual and distinct and wanted it to remain a clear part of my identity. I judged it would show an international dimension. It worked... My job in the FCO follows directly on... The fact that we are all (the group of 12) going to meet up (from different parts of the world) for a ten year reunion is quite extraordinary... Nothing of this kind was suggested by a single one of my year at school." A later GAPper, who claims he is a great fan of GAP and of those who run it, wrote: "Nearly everything I have done since my GAP year has been related to the experience and opportunities GAP offered me in China ... etc". Other diplomats found their skills had been learnt in GAP-China: "Many of the skills I used in my day to day life as a diplomat (in eastern Europe) were developed in China." Another who later spent time in Hangzhou learning the language and then three years in the Shanghai British Consulate-General, when asked the same question, replied succinctly, "All of it (her life)!" A doctor has written: "As far as the effect on my career, it has certainly featured in all my interviews as one of the things I am most proud of". Another could trace his call to the Bar to GAP: "It was a great year. There was the clear impact it would have on anyone, being the first time when one was 'away from home', but it has also slanted my entire outlook on life − positively I feel!" Hence after graduation he took a job at Swire's in Hong Kong. "While in HK my fascination with law also came to the fore − trying to work out the difference in lifestyles between the HK Chinese and mainland Cantonese − similar in nearly everything, save the rule of law. And so it is not at all far fetched to say that I am now embarking on a career as a barrister due in no small measure to GAP." A journalist in Hong Kong reported, "...I know I would not be doing what I am now doing or be in Hong Kong if I had not done GAP in China".

As already noted, many changed their degree courses to Chinese, or at least incorporated Chinese modules into their degrees. For one it went further. "Overall, I would say the GAP placement had a profound effect, as it resulted in me changing my university degree (to Chinese SOAS 2.1) in order to pursue my interest in Chinese and China. I also met my wife (a student at No.29 School, doing work experience in Xiwang Binguan) whilst on my placement, and have a nine month old baby daughter." A graduate with a First in psychology was so interested by the impact of Chinese medical procedures in the Traditional Chinese Medical (TCM) College, where she taught the lecturers and doctors English, that she wrote a doctoral thesis in relation to it: "My decision to do a PhD at Cambridge was strongly influenced by my experience in China..." ...At the TCM where they had strong contact with acupuncturists and other practitioners of Chinese medicine, "I was greatly impressed by the apparent efficiency of TCM which bore no relation to any of my teaching in Science in the west. However, as a scientist, I believed there must be a scientific, molecular basis for TCM, as yet undiscovered. TCM is holistic with a strong emphasis on mind-body interactions. I was therefore inspired to do a PhD studying the effects of stress (mind) on the brain (body)." Also, "Toughing it out in China for 6 months, aged 18, was one of the hardest things I have ever had to do. However, because of such a challenging experience, it has given me enormous confidence that I can cope with anything life may throw at me in the future."

For others it was the effect on their personalities and therefore indirectly on their career that predominated. "In some ways it was life-changing. It really challenged my values, because I was living in a society that seemed so different. I remember being homesick for England, but I was totally disorientated on my return to the UK." For another: "...while my experiences in China with GAP have not directly impacted on my life since, I changed a great deal out there, and came out a far stronger and better person. In some ways it was like a baptism of fire which I learnt from. Some experiences were pretty awful at the time... However, it taught me a lot about myself and looking back I would not change anything... I honestly believe that China and the whole experience of my year out changed my life. I'm fairly sure, having spoken to other GAP volunteers over the years, that my experience in Hangzhou (at the ZIT) was more difficult than that of others. I can accept that I may have been weak and unprepared, but, looking back, it was the hardship that I seemed to enjoy more than anything else and I feel it is this that has been of particular benefit to me... It seemed much longer but it was only the first few weeks that I hated. Looking back I think it was the isolation. I hadn't really got to know (my fellow GAPper) by then and there was no one else even to talk to... One night, perhaps in the second week, I cried myself to sleep. In the morning I got up and decided to smile. It was almost impossible to do, but I kept the smile. There have been instances since then when I have used the experience I gained in China to maintain my resolve. I have a strong belief, even today, that if I can get through that, I can get through anything". His partnership in Cairn Technology is "at least in part, thanks to GAP and China". For another it "was, however, a truly invaluable experience from a personal point of view. It may be a cliché to say so, that it was an eye-opening time which has shaped the person I am − I really believe so". One, a qualified engineer who has tried engineering and the City (investment banking) feels she is coming full circle to try some programme like GAP. "...I recognise how my experience in China has made me more attractive to prospective employers as well as making me a more rounded individual and I wholeheartedly encourage other teenagers and graduates to consider a similar opportunity." An academic lawyer, a university law lecturer, with a remarkable scholarly track record has written, "Despite all that has happened to me since China, I still feel the GAP year will be one of the seminal experiences of my life. It placed me in an extraordinarily challenging situation, which

124

tested my abilities in a way that has left me, I believe, able to cope with a great deal of pressure, responsibility and vulnerability, both in my personal and professional life". "…Going to China, at 19 to teach English with someone I barely knew and knowing that we had to stick it out for five whole months has in some way been the most important, impactful (and often impressive to others) event that has happened to me − it changed my life, my character, my outlook and now China is part of me whether through the news or my friend Richard who managed to escape a teaching career (in China) and learn accountancy in London…" One laconically remarked about the influence of a "fantastically organised programme" − "greater cultural awareness, more self-confidence, caught travel bug. More curiosity for foreign cultures".

**Changes in China**

Some noticed the massive change in China since the early 1990s. A former 1990 GAPper, a fluent Mandarin speaker, has noticed, "I now walk around the streets (in China) in awe of what has been achieved by such a massive country. When we first arrived (in 1990) everyone was using food coupons to get flour-based products and yoghurt, now you can buy as much as you want in international hypermarkets that even put Hong Kong to shame. I think this has helped me understand some of the quirks of the country, as I was able to experience a part of the modern evolution … but … as a non-Chinese I am never going fully to comprehend the place. …Our building (in Hangzhou), where we used to live, no longer exists; the school where we taught is also a distant memory. What were the outskirts of the city is now part of a sprawling metropolis. It (Hangzhou) really is a fascinating place now, but seems to have lost that sleepy charm of yesteryear − or is it just the fact that West Lake is now overshadowed by multi-storey building and pollution?"

Another volunteer of 1991 notes that at that time, he believed "China had a single American fast food restaurant, a

KFC in Beijing. Su tells me that Hangzhou (alone) now (2002) has over ten McDonalds and many other, similar types of food outlets. Apparently only a few weeks ago she went to the opening of Hangzhou's first Starbuck's. Perhaps this is a strange way to note how things have changed in China, but for me it says a lot".

## Final views

Several confess to pride in having done and completed the GAP experience. "The whole trip and time there was of much benefit to me. I think I am still most proud of the GAP year I took... I have no doubt it made me 'more diverse' (to quote the US expression) and allows me to be far less judgemental of other nationalities. The ability to communicate with (and) teach colleagues (and to show patience in the process)... To the extent we were placed so carefully, and looked after so discreetly, but yet left to think we were so detached, really helped to foster the desire to repeat the experience through more travel..." "China" wrote another "has taught me a lot. I have never been prejudiced, but I could never be racist now. The experience of living, befriending and experiencing a completely different culture and race, taught me that one's own perspective is also subjective, inadequate and incomplete... ...And, most importantly, the experience of living a completely different life has taught me to be thankful and not moan about what I have, and not to despair when things go badly. I can always begin afresh... ...I am proud to have been on GAP. It is one of my greatest achievements. I am proud to have been in Yueyang, where few foreigners had been by then (1994). I am proud to have returned by the Trans-Siberian Railway, and I am proud to have seen so many awesome places in China".

One who worked in Guangzhou, "not the most beautiful of the Chinese cities! (is) now working hard and (the GAP experience) seems light years away – great memories though". Another, a Hangzhou volunteer, reflects on the value of his experience: "I think China changed my life by giving (me) the belief that, if tested, I am very resilient. I've put myself to some testing situations since then, and have taken risks that have excited me rather than unnerved me. I would say that I have sought out such tests... ...The time I spent in China is still one of the proudest periods of my life. I was full of myself for quite some time on my return which I think was a negative response; older now, I keep the experience inside me, a reserve that I sometimes call on". One, now a merchant banker, echoes the comments of so many others; "I wouldn't change my China GAP experience for the world and feel it has probably benefited me in more ways than I will ever be aware of".

# 10. Conclusion

I gave up GAP-China's leading role in 1995, but I had not left the project altogether. Though I no longer had any dealings with the Chinese volunteers coming to the UK, nor any oversight over the original provinces of Jiangsu, Zhejiang and Fujian or over Qingdao City, my role as Project Manager of West China and CAAC was still fully occupied in looking after the placements in Sichuan (and later Yunnan) and the four CAAC colleges at Guangzhou, Shanghai, Guanghan and Tianjin.

As we have already seen, volunteers continued to go to Shanghai and Guangzhou, until I finally resigned in 1999. In Shanghai, additional work in the two middle schools, Jianjing in Changning district of the city, and Mingchang (founded 1928), enhanced GAP's role. Both of these were intriguing schools which would have been excellent to develop as separate placements, if only I myself had continued beyond 1999. In fact, I was already seriously considering negotiation with the Changning and Mingchang district *jiaoweis* about them. At CAAC's Flying College at Guanghan in Sichuan all went smoothly; nevertheless on my last visit in 1999 they told me that they had to terminate the arrangement − new CAAC headquarter regulations demanded a higher standard of aviation English for air traffic control, for which they would have to employ specialist instructors from professional air traffic control bodies abroad. Though the Guanghan connection consequently ended for sound reasons, it was sad for us. It had been a good placement, much liked by the GAPpers. Similarly, because GAP applicants for China as a whole had declined in number for October terms we could no longer fill the prestigious Tianjin placement for that semester each year. (CAAC and Rolls-Royce, if we had a shortfall of volunteers, insisted that Shanghai and Guangzhou must always have priority for English over the other two colleges.)

In Sichuan, apart from Guanghan, all was proceeding successfully. My relationship with Cai Li and Tan Jun at the

128

*jiaowei* flourished, and in 1997 they were joined by Yu Ying, an intellectually bright young woman with a top class degree in English. She became an efficient new official, fully fluent in English, and proved a great asset to GAP in those few years. Our placements at Neijiang Teachers' College and Chengdu No. 22 Middle School were a great success, both for the GAPpers and the institutions themselves. The three pairs of Sichuan GAPpers at Guanghan, Chengdu and Neijiang were geographically close enough to each other for them to meet at weekends in Chengdu, and yet not so near as to spoil the remote quality of GAP experience.

## Yunnan

Still keen to extend into the province of Yunnan, I set the necessary wheels in motion to this end in 1997. Some years earlier the British Council had told me how valuable GAP's entry into this south-west province would be. Its moderate climate (Yunnan means "south of the clouds" and Kunming its capital is dubbed "Spring City"), its geographical and ethnic diversity (50% of the population are non-Han Chinese) would make it attractive to our GAPpers, while they would be much in demand. On 21st October in that year (1997) I flew to Kunming with Yu Ying, who acted as the GAP interpreter, just as Du Jian, Gao Yuemin and Sun Hai Feng had done before elsewhere. Met by the Yunnan *jiaowei*, we visited Kunming Teachers' College, and also the Middle School attached to Yunnan Teachers' (called, as usual, "Normal") University and talked with the authorities in both places. Progress was, however, excruciatingly slow. Though I visited Kunming again the following May (1998), the *jiaowei waiban's* director was still abroad and I got no further, because his colleagues had failed to prepare the ground.

It was not until October that year that we at last made progress. This time I was with Jenny James, recently nominated to succeed me as West China Project Manager. The director of the *waiban* was now back from two years in Australia, and at last we had more substantive negotiations.

The two Kunming institutions I had visited earlier were still not ready for us, as major building programmes were in operation, but the *jiaowei* put us in touch with Dali Medical College which we visited and had productive talks at last; arrangements were made for the first GAPpers to start a year later, in October 1999. At this point Jenny had to return to the UK, and on my own I visited Yuxi Teachers' College some way south of Kunming; the town is famous – or infamous – all over China for the production of Hongtashan tobacco and cigarettes. We agreed for a placement there to start as soon as possible, in the following February (1999). I returned home after making fascinating private visits to Lhasa by air from Chengdu and to Hanoi by train from Kunming.

Jenny was unable to visit China in 1999, and I went instead. This May visit of mine to see the first two Yunnan volunteers at Yuxi, and to Dali Medical College to confirm arrangements for October were my last GAP visits before my final resignation. I arrived in Beijing just as the news was breaking of the American bombing of the Chinese Embassy in Belgrade. Not an ideal time to arrive, but though I saw the crowds protesting outside the US Embassy and later heard first hand from our consuls-general in Shanghai and Guangzhou of the threats to their offices, I received nothing but courtesy and friendship from officials and public alike wherever I went on trains, planes or in the streets.

Kunming's remarkable International Flower Festival also coincided with my visit which was interesting; there was a garden for every Chinese province and one each for most countries in the world. The UK was suitably represented by a beautifully designed red-bricked walled garden. I flew home by way of Yangon, Myanmar (Burma). Politically incorrect though this may have been, it was unforgettable; it revealed to me the fascination of the country and the quiet courtesy of the people. My project manager journeys were now over. Eleven years had passed since I was first appointed to set up and run the China project.

## The April 2001 Celebration

There was, however, on 5th April 2001, a final coda when I was invited to attend the tenth (in fact eleventh) year's celebration of the Project, held in Hangzhou on the banks of the West Lake in the impressive Xizi Hotel. Several hundred were present, including the Deputy Governor of Zhejiang Province, Nigel Cox; the Deputy Ambassador from the UK's Embassy in Beijing; many other officials, both British and Chinese; and from GAP itself, John Cornell; one of his deputies, Ed Bracher; my two successors, Michael Potter and Jenny James; and the GAP agents from the different provinces. There was a large number of GAPpers there too. It was a fitting end for me. John Cornell and I had begun with a mere six volunteers in 1990 – and here in 2001 was the fruit of all the work.

****

When I finally resigned, GAP-China had been running fully for nine years, though we started setting it up two years earlier in 1988. What had it achieved? Of what value had it been? In the early years there was for all of us something of the sense, the thrill, of the pioneering spirit. We all felt we were breaking new ground in China. Rarely, if ever, since 1949 had young British people worked for several months in China. In Fuzhou, for instance, in GAP-China's early years there were significantly only ten or a dozen other foreigners in the whole city, and these our GAPpers classed as elderly – not one was in their 20s or even perhaps 30s. In many places too, GAPpers were the first foreigners to have lived there at all, or to have been seen. Even as late as 1995, Neijiang students from the far-flung Sichuan countryside had never had previous contact with westerners.

The young GAPpers, conscientious and keen as they were, were, of course, inexperienced, but they nevertheless helped, we hope significantly, in the spread of spoken English language in China. For instance, as we have seen, the

131

principal of Qingdao No. 9 school spoke warmly of GAP's contribution to the school's immense leap in their standard of national English language examinations, and he was but one of many. For those working in teachers' colleges the potential effect was even greater, for each trainee teacher being taught by a GAPper would reach many thousands of pupils in a working life. One 1991 volunteer has written, in understatement, of the ripple effect. "In a teachers' college one GAPper", he estimated, "reaches 100 [student] teachers who then go on to instruct on average 750 pupils [a serious underestimate for a whole working life]. One GAPper reaches 750,000! Just think of the effect GAP has had on language teaching since 1990". But having GAPpers working in Chinese classrooms and extra-murally was not GAP's only contribution. By bringing young Chinese teachers of English to work in the UK for a whole year it enhanced their fluency in, and understanding of, English and their appreciation of UK culture. Consequently, all their future pupils in China flourished.

Nevertheless, I have had adverse criticism. It comes from British professional TEFL teachers who have worked in China, and who argue that pouring in many relatively untrained "school-leavers" dilutes and diminishes the reputation of the English-speaking professionals in the eyes of the Chinese. True, GAPpers are amateurs, they are young, and for the Chinese, cheap, but I refuse to accept the charge. The Chinese fully understand that we have never claimed our GAPpers to be fully-fledged language teachers, or anything more than mere teaching assistants who provide helpful support and the necessary native-spoken voice for the career Chinese teachers of English. GAPpers provide informal conversation after classroom hours which few older, long-term professionals would be keen to undertake. As I always told our Chinese principals and headmasters, just as our GAPpers were not professionals, nor were they mere run-of-the-mill school leavers. We selected them as leading high-grade "high school graduates" with places waiting for them at the top echelon of UK universities. We always chose them for their intellectual acumen and their ability to think on their feet, for they had to act nimbly in many classroom situations. They also happened to have been born with clearly-spoken English as their native tongue. In addition we were careful to choose them for skills in self-projection, proven in, for instance, school leadership roles, drama, debating, public speaking and giving instruction in sport, cadets or in other fields. Many were holders of Duke of Edinburgh awards, several at Gold level which is sufficient accolade in itself. In addition, as intelligent fast learners they had been able to absorb quickly, rudimentary teaching skills in the short one-week TEFL course in London before departure. With very few exceptions they responded magnificently. In any case, China is a vast place where there is plenty of room for both the professional TEFL teachers and our non-professional GAPpers.

For the GAPpers themselves the China experience, so they themselves say, not only enabled them to mature more quickly, thus allowing them to make better use of their university courses – it also taught them a new perspective on life. To have the eye-opening experience of living in an entirely different culture with a relative paucity of personal possessions, to learn how others live more simply in another country made a great impact on those brought up in our wealthy consumerist society. It gave them cause to reflect on their own situation. And yet getting to know and make friends with others in a different ethos made them realise that, at base, people of any culture, whatever their cultural differences, have the same or similar aspirations – at root, human beings are the same the world over, regardless of race or culture. For many the GAP experience opened up an entirely new interest – China with its language, its culture, its history, its social set-up and its economic base. For many of those, as we saw in chapter 9, it changed their whole lives, their choice of degree subject, their career and for a few even led to marriage across cultural boundaries.

In addition, the Chinese GAPpers coming to Britain had their chance of a year working in the UK. Though university level students and graduates, and even secondary school pupils, came with increasing frequency in the 1990s, there was little or no chance for young junior middle school teachers in their 20s to have such an experience. This benefited not only their schools and their future pupils, but themselves as people. It enhanced their experience of the world outside China, their self-confidence and their proficiency in English language.

Perhaps one of the greatest benefits was in building bridges, in creating friendships across the national divide and thus clearing mutual suspicion and misconceptions. When promoting the GAP experience in a new province, college or school, this was a point I stressed as a selling point for the project – if young people in both countries could establish friendships, they would not make the mistakes we and our forebears in the world have done in generating mistrust and creating international hostility. In our tiny way, GAP would be making a significant, if minuscule, contribution to promoting world peace for the future. As one 1991 volunteer, now a financial journalist, considered the worldwide impact of GAP, he recently wrote, "From a large geopolitical perspective the values of the organisation, like GAP, are ... much more evident in providing British students with an experience and knowledge of China wherever else they go, and keeping England involved with the world and in touch with what's going on. It also motivates some people, like myself, to further an interest sparked by the GAP experience. Interaction between people of different places and cultures is clearly very important; it might seem like fun, but after the events of September 11th (2001), the value of GAP is all the more apparent".

I am convinced that GAP-China will continue to flourish, especially under the vigorous leadership of my successor, Michael Potter, but it will only do so in new areas away from the large newly-rebuilt cosmopolitan cities. It is in fact now moving away from the westernised conurbations, the Hong Kong look-alikes, where it would atrophy. Times and perceptions change. In the early 1990s GAP-China was fantastically popular. Then, there was a mystification about China, leading to an abundant attraction for working there. Now it is no longer a place of mystery, of played-out Marxist economics, for so long shrouded from the gaze of the west. Furthermore, through the media, many western adolescents may mistakenly feel that China is yet another clutch of rather brash Hong Kong-like modern cities, and therefore not a true GAP period challenge. Though totally untrue of most of China, this misconception has nevertheless made GAP-China less popular for potential GAPpers than it was. GAP-China has an important continuing role to play, but there is little doubt that the period 1990 to 1995 was unique, unique in its pioneering spirit and unique in its reward.

# 11. Appendix.

## Some Memories of the Cultural Revolution

Over the years, several Chinese I met spoke to me of their memories of the Cultural Revolution and other events since 1949. They fell roughly into two groups – those who were already adult and working in 1966 when the Cultural Revolution was unleashed. I met several of these, the most notable of whom was, I suppose, a Catholic bishop, now in his mid-80's. He had been trained as a Jesuit, and completed his education in Rome before Liberation (1949), spending some time at the Jesuit college in Oxford. Returning home, he was ordained, but by 1955 he was under arrest for having been trained in Rome. For a long twenty-seven years he worked in a hard labour camp in the frozen north of China. He had no contact with the outside world, no books, not even a bible, breviary, or missal. He could not say Mass, except in his head. He remarkably survived until 1982, when he was released and was ordained bishop. Before his release he knew nothing of the outside world. He had not heard of Pope John XXIII nor of the great changes brought about by the Second Vatican Council of the early 1960s. A short man with twinkling eyes, his mind is sharp, he is fluent in five languages, and is thoroughly ecumenical in his approach to others. He implemented the Vatican II changes; Mass is in Mandarin with the new liturgy. Most significant of all he bears no bitterness. "The past is the past; push it aside. I look to the future always". A remarkable witness of great resilience and cheerfulness. His great reward is to see the rapidly expanding ranks of young priests and the burgeoning congregations in his city.

Almost as significant are those on whom in the long term the impact was greatest, those whose early years were totally disrupted, their education devastated. These would have been between ten and eighteen years of age at the Cultural Revolution (1966-1976). A university professor told me in

1994 that those then aged 38 or 39 had had the hardest time – they lost their education. I thought of several of my first GAP colleagues and friends who were just of that age. They had had to educate themselves – and pull themselves up by their bootstraps. Many failed to do so and remained as manual workers. The ones I had met had shown great courage and self-discipline. The names given here are not their real names.

**** 

Helen (her English name) and I were travelling in an official car driven by a driver with no English, so we could talk freely. Trying to be polite, I said how much I thought Chairman Mao had done for China and its people; he had redistributed wealth and made the country self-sufficient. "Nonsense," Helen said. "He did so much harm. He ruined my family. My grandparents were very wealthy merchants in Chongqing, trading for generations with British, French and other Europeans. They had a large, well-furnished house, and were able to bring up sixteen children, all well nourished and educated. Then came 'Liberation'. My grandfather had the choice of either giving all his possessions and wealth to the state and living as a free man – or of going to prison, and whatever future the state decided. He gave all to the state – and lived in poverty until his death. His son, my father, and his wife, my mother, were highly educated and great experts on Chinese culture. That became a problem for them at the Cultural Revolution. The Red Guards got hold of my parents and arrested them. I shall never forget some days later when I was taken to our school assembly hall with my school fellows, and there on the platform were my father and mother with placards hanging round their necks, being harangued as 'Guomintang traitors'. I had to try to show no emotion, I had to repress all my feelings – or be a traitor myself. I held myself in. Even today, 27 years later, I frequently wake in the night screaming after horrific nightmares. That will always be with me. It has done permanent damage."

****

Another spoke of how he entered university in 1965, became an active Red Guard, went to Tiananmen for a parade, saw Mao, was so excited and returned to his hometown, but his father was "a well-known chef" and was thus condemned as a "bourgeois liberal". The young man soon decided to stop being a Red Guard; his excuse being that his grandmother was ill. Nevertheless he was later, in 1968, sent to the fields "for education" miles away and also worked on the Yangtze Bridge. Thus he never completed his university course, and his career had been ruined.

****

Zhang Yuan, a Sichuanese, born in 1952, told me that his father was a Guomintang military doctor, and his mother was also a doctor. "At Liberation (1949) my father became a civilian doctor and eventually rose to be Dean of Medicine at Chongqing, but even at this stage at primary school I was treated badly, as I was branded as one of 'One of the Black Nines' (landlords, etc.) – so I had no chance. When the Cultural Revolution arrived in 1966 when I was 14, I could not be a Red Guard; I was initially saved because my father was Dean of Medicine. Nevertheless I had to pretend I agreed with the Red Guards, though I thought the Little Red Book was absolutely mad. I eventually escaped to Qinghai province near Tibet for two years and worked with relatives on a farm. My father, the Dean of Medicine, was soon made to work in fields, but he suffered from hypertension, from which he later died. In the 1970s I returned to my *danwei* (work unit), the medical university, first as a sweeper, then as a lab assistant. Yet I was still prevented from being a medical student which I wanted to be, because I was still classed as 'Black Nine'. Nevertheless I gained experience in pathology, cutting up bodies and so on. Then I managed to gain entry to the Foreign Language Institute and achieved a degree in English, after which I had a job in the *waiban* of the Medical University

138

where I met students from the UK, especially the Middlesex Hospital. Since then I have worked at the Sichuan *jiaowei*, and in a bank. My wife still lives in Chongqing with a nine year old daughter."

****

Li Feng, born in 1952 or 1953, told me he came from a poor family in Shaoxing. Liberation in 1949 gave him his chance to escape from poverty. Nevertheless he suffered between the ages of 13 and 16 in the Cultural Revolution. He was sent sixty miles from home into the countryside to work. On his return he had to work in a factory for two years. All this was very worrying for his family. He started studying on his own to take the entrance exam to university. He failed in 1977, but passed in the next year, and entered the university. After getting his degree, he worked on the *waiban* of the *jiaowei*, where, like all education officials in 1991, he was working six days a week and, since the troubles in 1989, had had no holidays. He later in the 91/92 won an award and took his MA at Sussex University.

****

Surrounded as we were at the seaside at Xiamen by an excited group of primary school children up from the countryside for the day, Ho Wei suddenly exclaimed, "How lucky they are to have a happy childhood like that!"

"You mean with no cultural revolution?"

"No, not that. It was well beforehand – Mao's Great Leap Forward in 1962. I was only eight years old – and we were starving. All we had to eat as a family was grass and weeds. Many of us faced, and were near to, death.

"At the age of 13 (1966), I was sent to the fields for ten years. My two younger sisters were not yet in middle school, so they did not go. Several of those of us in the country took books and tried to keep our education going, but many did not. It was not until the age of 23 I was able to leave the fields. By 25 I had achieved entry to university (1978) for a degree in English. About ten years later I went to Swansea University and took an MA degree." This was a remarkable show of resilience.

**\*\*\*\***

A senior official told me "I was responsible as one of the Red Guards for helping to tear down the beautiful ancient Gate in the centre of Chengdu where the statue of Chairman Mao now stands — and in the following year the ancient town walls. I much regret it all." When he took me to the Jin Jiang Hotel for a meal, he told me of the rally in that very dining room and nearby. He said, "As a young boy, I had to stand on one of the roofs and peer through one of the upper windows on the centre of the rally inside. How different it is now."

**\*\*\*\***

Mary, her English name, born in 1963, was one of the first six Chinese GAPpers to come to the UK in 1990/1. We met again in November 1994 and we discussed her earlier experiences. "When I was thirteen in 1966, I was sent away to work for three years. On my return home at the age of 17 I had to heave myself up the educational ladder. In the last year of the Cultural Revolution from 1972 onwards, people only went to university for political reasons not for academic ability, but I did not want to get involved in political activities. In 1972 I was asked if I wanted to be a teacher. To be a teacher was the last thing I wanted to do. I went to a country school where the standard was low and I was getting nowhere. Nevertheless I was chosen to go to a teachers' college where they train teachers for both primary and junior secondary schools, but I did so well in the exams that I was chosen to go to the Teachers' University to train for senior secondary school teachers. Really, however, I did not then want to be a teacher at all, but to get a good academic degree and use it for another career. Really though I am now glad with what I've done.

"I found the last years of the Cultural Revolution to be a 'wonderful, beautiful time', where everybody was working for the good of others. As a young Red Guard, I remember as part of my service I had to take water every day to elderly people in the countryside, and I liked doing that. Nowadays it is horrible compared; everybody is going for money, going for what they can get. In some ways I still long for the attitudes of those last days of the Cultural Revolution. I was too young in 1966 to 1969 to remember the terrible, mindless violence, which I deplore, but there really was something beautiful about the last stage of the Cultural Revolution with its ideal of serving others." I asked whether others felt like that. "Yes, quite a lot." Then we had quite a discussion on the merits and demerits of Capitalism, full Socialism and Socialism with Chinese Characteristics.

142

Printed in the United Kingdom
by Lightning Source UK Ltd.
98810UKS00001B/105-148